Gail Zander
May 1981

Smith College Studies in History
Volume XLVIII

SMITH COLLEGE STUDIES IN HISTORY
VOLUME XLVIII IN HONOR OF
PHYLLIS WILLIAMS LEHMANN

NORTHAMPTON MASSACHUSETTS
M · C · M · L · X · X · X

LIBRARY OF CONGRESS CATALOG CARD NUMBER 80–53219
ISBN 87391–019–2

The Smith College Studies in History are published at irregular intervals and may be ordered from: Order Department, Smith College Library, Northampton, Massachusetts 01063

TABLE OF CONTENTS

Introduction
ELIZABETH GALLAHER VON KLEMPERER
page 9

The Ancients' Concept of Antiquity
JUSTINA GREGORY
page 13

Changing Images of Cicero in the Early Italian Renaissance
JOACHIM W. STIEBER
page 27

Palladio and Antiquity
PHYLLIS WILLIAMS LEHMANN
page 49

The Landscape of Allusion: Literary Themes in the Gardens of Classical Rome and Augustan England
JOHN PINTO
page 97

The Founding Fathers and Antiquity: A Selective Passion
LOUIS COHN-HAFT
page 137

Homer and the Twentieth Century
KENNETH CONNELLY
page 157

INTRODUCTION

Wherever the search for our biological roots may take us, our cultural roots lie partly in Greece and Rome. These roots have been rediscovered again and again—by fourteenth-century Italians, by seventeenth-century Englishmen, by the founding fathers of the United States, by twentieth-century expatriates. The ideas, myths, and images of Greek philosophers, poets, and sculptors, of Roman legislators and builders, have borne new fruit again and again, sometimes in places that would have seemed remote even to Odysseus or the emperor Hadrian.

Indeed the culture of classical antiquity was flourishing modestly a hundred years ago in Northampton, Massachusetts. Lecturing in America in 1883–1884, the English man of letters Matthew Arnold remarked that "women will study Greek, as Lady Jane Grey did; I believe that in that chain of forts, with which the fair host of the Amazons are now engirdling our English universities, [and] I find that here in America, in colleges like Smith College in Massachusetts . . . they are studying it already."

Today, although only a stalwart few successors of Smith's first "fair Amazons" read Homer in the original, ancient Greece and Rome continue to influence the curriculum of the College, often indirectly, sometimes with an exciting immediacy. For generations of students this immediacy, this distinct presence of the ancient past, was created memorably by Phyllis Williams Lehmann, William J. Kenan, Jr. Professor of Art, whose career as archeologist and scholar has shown compellingly how the shape and also the vital meaning of ancient monuments can be rediscovered. When Mrs. Lehmann retired in 1978, her colleagues honored her by holding a distinguished loan exhibition, "Antiquity in the Renaissance," in the Smith College Museum of Art. Fittingly, the program of the 1978 session of Alumnae College, "The Survival of Antiquity," was centered on that exhibition. The six lectures given on this occasion by members of the Smith Faculty constitute this—the forty-eighth volume of the *Smith College Studies in History*.

Readers of the lectures reproduced here will find of interest the catalogue of the Museum's exhibition containing a fine introductory essay by Wendy Sheard, who organized the exhibition while guest curator at Smith College in 1977–1978. Like Mrs. Sheard's essay, the lectures in this volume deal with relationships between classical cultures and the art or thought of other epochs. Justina Winston Gregory's lecture reminds us that the Greeks themselves looked back to a past epoch, from which they derived inspiration or again a warning. Mrs. Lehmann's lecture deals with a great Renaissance architect's use of antique models, and Joachim Stieber's with the political implications—strangely pertinent to the twentieth century—of changing images of Cicero in the Renaissance. The other lectures deal with uses of ancient culture in more recent epochs, including our own.

The lectures in this volume suggest, then, the various ways in which a culture survives. "Survival" is of course a two-faced word. We often associate it with endangered things, with species, customs, languages, artifacts menaced or in fact almost destroyed by hostility or indifference or mere time. But we also associate "survival" with those things that endure, with institutions, monuments, ideas, images so strong that they resist the vicissitudes of history, or else so valuable that they are somehow preserved—or, if lost, sought until they are recovered.

ELIZABETH GALLAHER VON KLEMPERER

THE ANCIENTS' CONCEPT OF ANTIQUITY

The Ancients' Concept of Antiquity

JUSTINA GREGORY

FOR MOST OF US it is a genuine pleasure to contemplate the past. Agreeable memories readily present themselves, while little seems required in the way of attitude or judgment. Yet this same act of retrospection, on further thought, invites questions. How, exactly, do we understand the past? Does it have a life of its own or exist only in our own perceptions of it? Do we enjoy looking backward because the past was better than the present or, paradoxically, because it was worse? What are the uses of the past, and will it help or hinder us to invoke it?

Such questions are implicit in every reminiscence, but pose themselves with especial poignancy, perhaps, to those who find themselves back at Smith at reunion time. What I should like to do this evening is to consider the past within a specific cultural context: to turn to the past of classical antiquity and consider how the ancients, reflecting on their own history, chose to answer some of the questions I have just raised. From the literature of the Greeks and Romans we can hope to gain a perspective which will enable us, in turn, to integrate our pasts with our present.

As old as the oldest literature we possess is the notion that better times lay just before. The *Iliad* and the *Odyssey* stand at the beginning of the Western literary tradition. To our modern eyes they seem bright with archaic splendor, evoking, in the words of John Finley, a "world lit by a kind of six-o'-clock-in-the-morning light and the dew imperishably on the grass."[1] Yet the inhabitants of the Homeric world were far from believing that they stood at the beginning; they seem, indeed, often to have felt that they came at the end. Nestor in particular, the venerable king of Pylos who has seen two generations arise, flourish, and die, is struck by the inferiority of his present companions to the associates of his youth:

1. John Finley, *Four Stages of Greek Thought* (Stanford, 1965), p. 2.

> . . . in my time
> men who were even greater have I known
> and none of them disdained me. Men like those
> I have not seen again, nor shall: Perithoös,
> the Lord Marshal Dryas, Kaineus, Exadios,
> Polyphemos, Theseus—Aigeus' son,
> a man like the immortal gods. I speak
> of champions among men of earth, who fought
> with champions, with wild things of the mountains,
> great centaurs whom they broke and overpowered.
> Among these men I say I had my place
> when I sailed out of Pylos, my far country,
> because they called for me. I fought
> for my own hand among them. Not one man
> alive now upon earth could stand against them.[2]

Nestor is addressing himself to Agamemnon and Achilles. Agamemnon may be the king of men and Achilles the best of the Achaeans—these are the regular epithets they enjoy in the poem—but they are a disappointment to Nestor. And Nestor speaks for a tradition. The sense that the men of some former time were bigger, stronger, and more vital becomes, with time, habitual in Greek literature. It persists down to the Roman era, where we find Lucretius offering a tentative explanation. Originally, he explains, men were born from the earth, so they were hard like their mother, and fresh and strong like her:

> The race of men was much sturdier then in the land, as one would expect, since the hard earth had created it. Men had larger and more solid bones, and stronger sinews . . . they were not easily harmed by heat or cold or strange food or any disease.[3]

Now, however, the earth is worn out, too old for childbearing.[4] Lucretius seems here to assimilate the tradition of the degeneration of mankind to his own picture of the senescence of the earth. His ideas have their ancestry in the *Iliad*. And this sense of a gradual enfeeblement over the course of time, along with a pervasive consciousness of mortality, touches the Homeric dawn with untimely shadow.

The men of former times were not only physically bigger and stronger, but morally superior as well. The Homeric poems have war as their backdrop, and the heroes aim for military prowess and the public recognition that will go with it. The lyric poetry of the centuries

2. *Iliad,* I, 260–272 (trans. by Robert Fitzgerald, Garden City, 1976). This and subsequent classical passages reflecting on the past are collected by Arthur O. Lovejoy and George Boas, *Primitivism and Related Ideas in Antiquity* (Baltimore, 1935).

3. Lucretius, V, 925–930.

4. Lucretius, V, 826–827.

following, however, addresses itself to more private concerns, articulating standards appropriate to civilian life. The poet Theognis, who lived in the sixth century B.C., draws an implicit contrast between the past, when moral standards were still in force, and the decadent present when

> Only the good goddess Hope still lives on earth; the others have gone off to Olympus. The great goddess Good Faith has departed, and Decency, and the Graces have left the earth, and just oaths are no longer honored, and no one has respect for the immortal gods. The race of pious men is gone by. . . .[5]

The context of this passage is not certain; we can only guess that it was inspired by some vivid sense of personal injury. But when the poet generalizes his experience to declare that the fault (whatever it may have been) lies with the times, he is not just taking refuge in a convenient cliche. His lines reflect a deeply rooted pessimism about the way civilization is tending. Such an attitude is not uncommon in poetry of the pre-Classical period; it is, indeed, almost the necessary complement to the belief that things had been better in some former time.

The men of the past were stronger, then, and more virtuous. But they were also, and here is the crux of the matter, far happier. Hesiod, who lived in the seventh century B.C., is the author of a poem entitled *Works and Days*—a strangely miscellaneous text touching not only on farming, sailing, and the necessity of work but also on piety, rectitude, and the evil of unproductive strife. The poem also includes a stylized account of the successive ages of mankind. Hesiod describes five generations, of which the first was the Golden Age:

> First of all the immortal gods made a golden race of men. . . . They lived like gods themselves, carefree, apart from toil and grief. They never knew the miseries of old age, but remained strong in hands and feet and rejoiced in feasts and were strangers to any misfortune. And when they died, it was as if they had fallen asleep.[6]

Though not immortal, the men of the Golden Age seem to escape the suffering attendant on mortality. They are spared the infirmities of advancing age, and death comes gently and peacefully. They do not even do any work because, as Hesiod informs us, "the generous earth bore fruit for them of its own accord, lavishly and without stint."[7] Under these circumstances they are perfectly free from anxiety, and enjoy, as Hesiod remarks, the very condition of the gods.

Hesiod's picture of a Golden Age where the earth bore food spon-

5. Theognis, *Elegies*, I, 1135–1142.
6. Hesiod, *Works and Days*, 109–116.
7. Hesiod, *Works and Days*, 117–118.

taneously seems to have taken a hold on the Greek imagination. There are echoes of it in Euripides' *Bacchae*, where the Bacchantes who have abandoned Thebes for the mountains have only to strike the ground with their staffs for streams of milk, wine, and honey instantly to well forth. The traditional Golden Age was simple and vegetarian, but the picture could also be absurdly elaborated, as in this parody by the fifth-century comic writer Teleclides:

> At the beginning there was universal peace. . . . And the earth knew neither fear nor disease, and all the necessities appeared of their own accord. Every stream flowed with wine, and barley cakes fought with wheat cakes to enter the mouths of men, begging to be gulped down. . . . And fishes came to men's houses and baked themselves, and then served themselves at table. And a river of soup flowed by the couches, swirling hot meats along with it, and pipes conducting savory sauces ran alongside. . . . And there were pancakes elbowing each other aside at one's mouth, and shouting their war cries. . . .[8]

Unfortunately these delightful beginnings did not endure. We cannot fail to notice a degeneration in Hesiod's account of the five ages of man. The Golden Age is succeeded by a generation of silver: these men endure a childhood lasting up to a hundred years, and their brief and violent adulthood is followed by untimely death. The men of the third generation, the Age of Bronze, destroy themselves by their aggressive temperaments, for war is the only occupation they know. The fourth and only non-metallic age, the brave and just generation which comprises the Age of Heroes, brings a temporary improvement. But the men of the fifth or iron age, Hesiod's own, eke out the hardest existence of all. "Neither by day do they pause from toil and sorrow," reports Hesiod, "nor by night from wasting away"[9]—and he grimly predicts that things will get worse before they get better.

No reason is offered for this degeneration. The Roman writers, in a moralizing vein, sometimes theorize that man has incurred divine punishment through his own audacity, his refusal to acknowledge natural limits. As Horace put it:

> Nothing is too difficult for mortals. We storm heaven itself in our folly, and such is our wickedness that we do not let Jupiter lay down his angry thunderbolt.

> nil mortalibus ardui est:
> caelum ipsum petimus stultitia neque
> per nostrum patimur scelus
> iracunda Jovem ponere fulmina.[10]

8. Teleclides, *Amphictyons* in Athenaeus, *Deipnosophistai*, VI, 268. Translation based on that of Lovejoy and Boas (above, n. 2).

9. Hesiod, *Works and Days*, 176–178.

10. Horace, *Odes*, I.3 37–40.

Hesiod offers no such explanation—a circumstance which only deepens the atmosphere of gloom, for where there is no understanding there can be no remedy. We might link this sense of gloom to the melancholy that cast its shadow over Homer, to the pessimism of Theognis, and to a general archaic sense that men can exercise only the most tenuous control over their destinies. A man's fate was allotted to him at birth: it might contain good mixed with evil, or possibly just evil, but never unalloyed good.[11] His lot was to grow old in the company of this destiny, in a world which, moreover, was also subject to aging and degeneration.

That is a somber view of human existence, to be sure; but it is also a whole and unified one. There is something admirable, and quintessentially classical, in the archaic tendency to link individual destiny to the human condition and the human condition to the very pattern of the universe, including the world and the mortals who tenant it in a single unflinching vision.

The following centuries, while retaining this wholeness of vision, turned away from archaic pessimism as from many other traditional attitudes. The sixth and fifth centuries before Christ saw enormous advances in knowledge and the accompanying emergence of new intellectual dispositions. To take only a few random examples: with advances in astronomy it became possible to predict eclipses of the sun. With advances in physics the laws of conservation of energy and matter, the theory of gravity, and atomic theory were all predicated. With advances in medicine the effects on health of diet and environment were studied and techniques of clinical observation established. Such developments must have gone far to render the natural world more intelligible, less seemingly random and frightening.

Social developments kept step with advances in knowledge. The fifth century witnessed the establishment in Athens of a radical democracy that assumed no natural hierarchies among men, no inborn division between governors and governed. Men could take confidence in themselves, and begin to shake off fatalism. No longer need they assume that their destinies had been allotted at birth; instead they could feel free to develop themselves through instruction, enhancing natural abilities with those acquired skills that the Greeks called *technai*. A would-be tragedian, for instance, could supplement the Muses' inspiration by such handbooks as Sophocles' manual on the Chorus; the apprentice architect could read Ictinus' essay on the Parthenon, or Hippodamus of Miletus' manual on city planning.

The transmission of knowledge was not limited to handbooks. One

11. *Iliad*, XXIV, 527–533.

could also take courses. From the mid-fifth century on there gathered in Athens a group of professional teachers qualified to provide instruction in a wide range of subjects. These were the notorious Sophists, who at once mirror and help create the intellectual atmosphere of the time.

The Sophists were not members of a school; each had his specialty and lived and worked quite independently. Nevertheless we sense in them certain shared approaches and assumptions. They were willing to instruct anyone who could meet their rather high fees—that is, they did not believe that intellectual attainment was an inborn and restricted gift. Along with their various specialties, most offered instruction in rhetoric, for it was rhetoric that would help an ambitious young Athenian make his mark in the assembly or the law court. The Sophists imparted useful, practical techniques for discrediting one's opponent and presenting one's own case in the best possible light, for arguing on either side of a question without much regard to truth or falsehood.

It is easy to condemn the Sophists for their mercenary approach to education and their relentlessly relativistic handling of ethical controversies. But we should not underestimate the importance of their assumption that men can learn, through instruction, to direct their own lives. The Sophists seem to have formed the focus for an optimistic assessment of human capabilities and an enthusiastic appreciation of human achievements.

It is therefore not surprising that in the circle of the Sophists we find articulated, in opposition to the culture's traditional beliefs, a doctrine of progress: a view that sees the present as better than the past, not worse, and anticipates that the future will be better still. The Sophists began with the perception that the life of early man, far from being a Golden Age of peace and abundance, must have been very unpleasant indeed. Naked against the elements and lacking natural means of defence, man was worse off than the animals. It was sheer necessity that drove him to band together in societies and to remedy his lacks. At first he found only the most elementary solutions for the most pressing needs: clothes, housing, basic agricultural techniques. Later he moved beyond these achievements to develop the *technai*, the arts and skills that make for culture.[12]

There are various theories to account for the gradual improvements in human life. Democritus asserts that men took instruction from the birds and beasts, imitating the spider's weaving and spinning, the swallow's house-building, the swan and the nightingale's singing.[13] Other ac-

12. Cf. Plato, *Protagoras*, 320 d ff., Diodorus, I. 8 1–7, and the discussion of theories of progress in W. K. C. Guthrie, *The Sophists* (Cambridge, 1969), 60–84 (= *A History of Greek Philosophy*, Vol. III, Part I).

13. Fr. 154 Diels-Kranz.

counts assign an influential role to some semi-divine culture hero: Prometheus, the bringer of fire, or Palamedes, the inventor of number.[14] Still others suggest that it was the gods themselves who taught men such skills as agriculture, navigation, and commerce.[15] But all the accounts are in agreement that it was man, through his aided or unaided efforts, who brought about change, and that each change was for the better. "The gods did not reveal to men all things from the beginning," says Xenophanes (no Sophist, as it happens, but a sixth-century precursor), "but men through their own search found in the course of time that which was better."[16]

Such an emphasis on human achievement and on improvement over time is in strong contrast to the theory of the Golden Age. A second look, however, reveals that both pictures are based on the same evidence: they embody two different perceptions of the same state. Hesiod's Golden Age, where the earth bore food spontaneously, is identical to the Sophists' pre-agricultural society where men were food-gatherers rather than farmers. If the Golden Age knew no work it was only because—in the view of the Sophists—men did not yet have tools to work with or understand what labor could accomplish. In short, the miserable primitive state described by the Sophists is simply Hesiod's Golden Age viewed through a cold anthropological eye that sees deprivation where Hesiod saw abundance, crudeness where Hesiod saw simplicity.

That attitude affects perception in these matters is amusingly confirmed by a passage from Plato's *Republic*. Socrates has just finished describing his ideal community: the citizens recline on yew and myrtle boughs and spread their food before them: barley-cakes, olives, cheese, figs, peas, beans. . . . At this Glaucon, a refined young aristocrat, exclaims in disgust: "If you were establishing a city for pigs, Socrates, how would you organize things any differently?"[17]

If one man's Golden Age is another's city of pigs, then we seem to have come round at last to one of our initial questions: does the past have an independent existence, or does it depend on our own continual reinterpretation? Clearly there is nothing fixed about a past which can be interpreted so variously by subsequent ages or even viewed so differently by two contemporaries, such as Socrates and Glaucon. And clearly so fluid and elusive a past requires our constant reappraisal.

To turn now to our second question, which concerned the uses of the

14. Prometheus: Aeschylus, *Prometheus Bound*, 442–468, 476–506. Palamedes: Nauck², Frag. Adespota 470.

15. Euripides, *Suppliant Women*, 201–213.

16. Xenophanes, Fr. 18 Diels-Kranz.

17. Plato, *Republic*, 372 a–d.

past. Again, different eras offered different answers. The archaic age found in the celebration of the past not so much a benefit accruing to the rememberers as a duty owed to the remembered. Such an assumption is reflected in the *Iliad*, where fighting is made endurable by the belief that it will bring fame after death. Achilles, the youthful hero of the *Iliad*, has been warned that he must choose between two outcomes:

> My mother, Thetis of the silvery feet,
> tells me of two possible destinies
> carrying me toward death: two ways:
> if on the one hand I remain to fight
> around Troy town, I lose all hope of home
> but gain unfading glory; on the other,
> if I sail back to my own land my glory
> fails—but a long life lies ahead for me.[18]

Achilles' is no special case; his choice only crystallizes the situation of every other warrior at Troy. For each of them fame is the one sure means of survival, and reputation won on the battlefield is the only way of transcending, if any mortal can, the limits of mortality. "Unfading glory" is the reward of heroism: a life well lived, whether short or long, will be celebrated in song forever.

To remember the past is to render due honor to those who lived well and died well. But it is also a negative or custodial measure. Because Greece of the Heroic Age had lost the art of writing, oral tradition was an important repository of past events. To let the past lapse from memory was to risk consigning it to oblivion—a risk no one was eager to take. The historian Herodotus, though a man of the fifth century, preserves the archaic point of view in some important respects. In the opening of his *Histories* he combines both motives for remembering the past, the positive and the negative, the honorific and the custodial:

> These are the investigations of Herodotus of Halicarnassus, which he sets forth so that the deeds of men shall not grow faded through time, and so that the great and wonderful accomplishments of Greeks and barbarians alike shall not lose the honor due them. . . .[19]

As writing came into use once again and men began to understand that the past could be preserved on wax or clay, marble or bronze, the task of remembering came to seem less urgent. In keeping with the more practical outlook and the altered focus of the new age, the men of the fifth century tended to value the past not for the sake of another's honor but for their own self-interest; and less with a view to preserving what

18. *Iliad*, IX, 410–416 (trans. by Robert Fitzgerald, Garden City, 1976).
19. Herodotus, I, 1.

had gone before than to predicting what was yet to come. It seemed, in this connection, possible to forge a link between the past and the future.

The future had, of course, also been of interest to archaic man: it had long been the practice to consult the flight of birds or the entrails of sacrificial animals for some indication of what the gods might have in store. But implicit in these procedures was the assumption that the future was the domain of the gods, not of men. The Sophists, in contrast, held that the future was subject to individual control, and set out to construct models of human responses to possible future situations, prognostications based on theories of what, given human nature, was probable or likely. They found no better means of refining the accuracy of their prognostications than by studying the past.

Thucydides offers an example. A near-contemporary of Herodotus, Thucydides seems almost to belong to another era, so imbued is he with advanced ideas. He embarks on his own *Histories* with a purpose very different from Herodotus':

> It may well be that my story will seem less easy to read because of the absence of a romantic element. It will be enough for me, however, if my work is judged useful by those who want to understand clearly the events which happened in the past and which, human nature being what it is, will at some time or other and in much the same ways be repeated in the future.[20]

The Romans found still another use for the past. Less given to abstraction than the Greeks, they tended to see history as a procession of individuals, virtuous or wicked, failures or successes. The Augustan historian Livy suggests that his readers should look for *exempla* or models of conduct:

> I invite the reader's attention to the consideration of the kind of lives our ancestors led—of who were the men, and what the means both in politics and war by which Rome's power was first acquired and subsequently expanded; I would have him trace the process of our moral decline, to watch, first, the sinking of the foundations of morality as the old teaching was allowed to lapse, then the rapidly increasing degeneration, then the final collapse of the whole edifice and the dark dawning of our modern day when we can neither endure our vices nor face the remedies needed to cure them.[21]

We may notice that for Livy, in the first century B.C., the old theory of degeneration has returned in force! But that is not the point. The point is that Livy sees history as offering a series of models for conduct:

> The study of history is the best medicine for a sick mind, for in history you have a record of the infinite variety of human experience plainly set out for all to see;

20. Thucydides, 1.22 4 (trans. by Rex Warner, New York, 1972).
21. Livy, *Praefatio*, 9 (trans. by Aubrey de Selincourt, New York, 1971).

and in that record you can find for yourself and your country both examples and warnings: fine things to take as models, base things to avoid.[22]

"Find for yourself and your country . . .": the classical wholeness of vision which was able to embrace at once the world and an individual's place in it is still intact.

The past seems to have held a higher place of honor among the ancients than it does for us. That is not to say, however, that they were ignorant of the dangers inherent in the retrospective attitude. Hesiod is the author, in addition to the *Works and Days*, of a poem called the *Theogony* which recounts the genealogy of the gods. He reports that Mnemosyne, the Goddess of Memory, gave birth to the Muses in union with Zeus, "to be a forgetfulness (*lēsmosunē*) of evils and a rest from anxieties."[23] His juxtaposition of memory and forgetfulness suggests, I think, that the mind operates selectively, and that one chooses to remember one thing at the expense of another. Livy, for one, quite candidly admits that his historical studies divert him from the present:

I find antiquity a rewarding study, if only because, while I am absorbed in it, I shall be able to turn my eyes from the troubles which for so long have tormented the modern world. . . .[24]

We may say, in summary, that for the archaic age the study of the past offered a bulwark against forgetfulness; for the later Greeks, a key to the future; for the Romans, models of conduct in the present. But what is the past to us, or what should it be? I do not think that we can draw on the past as the Sophists or the Romans proposed to. If we pursue to its limit Thucydides' assumption that human nature will always be the same, we will find ourselves enmeshed in a kind of psychological determinism no less constricting than the archaic fatalism from which his age was struggling to get free. As for the Roman idea that history offers models of conduct, we are now, I believe, reluctant to revert to so rudimentary a notion either of history or of human behavior.

There remains the archaic notion of the past as reminder, and this idea, I suspect, still offers us a good deal of meaning. No less today than in the archaic age does the past deserve honor for its own sake. Indeed, it is precisely today, when we have so many technical means of preservation at our disposal, that the past is in greatest danger of extinction. To reduce knowledge to a magnetic image which is then stored in a computer memory is more truly an act of forgetting than remembering, for as we perform this process we simultaneously dismiss the material from our minds. It is only by the constant recollection of what we have

22. Livy, *Praefatio*, 10 (trans. by Aubrey de Selincourt, New York, 1971).
23. Hesiod, *Theogony*, 53–55.
24. Livy, *Praefatio*, 5 (trans. by Aubrey de Selincourt, New York, 1971).

observed that we stand any chance of profiting from our experiences; it is only by the constant reconsideration of past events that we stand any chance of learning from them. Our world has lost the classical sense of wholeness: we can no longer achieve the ancients' synthesis between private and public, individual and generic. Under the circumstances the need to exercise our memories is, I think, greater than ever before. We must look to the past to restore some of our lost perspective. There is no need to pass judgment on the past, as the ancients did, assessing it as either better or worse than the present. But we have, as they did, an obligation to remember—an activity which turns out to be far more difficult, but also more fruitful, than it had at first seemed.

We ought, finally, to keep in mind, as the Greeks did, that without remembering there can be no truth. That at least is what is suggested by the etymology of the Greek word *alētheia*. The French scholar Marcel Detienne has suggested that *alētheia*, truth, is the term for forgetfulness, *Lēthē*, with a negative prefix: it means, then, "Lack of *Lēthē*," or "non-forgetting."[25] And if truth is non-forgetting, then it may well be that the only way to arrive at some vision—however flawed, however fleeting—of the world and our own place in it is through the periodic contemplation of the past.

25. Marcel Detienne, "La Notion Mythique d''Αλήθεια," *REG* 73, 1960, 27–35.

CHANGING IMAGES OF CICERO IN THE EARLY ITALIAN RENAISSANCE

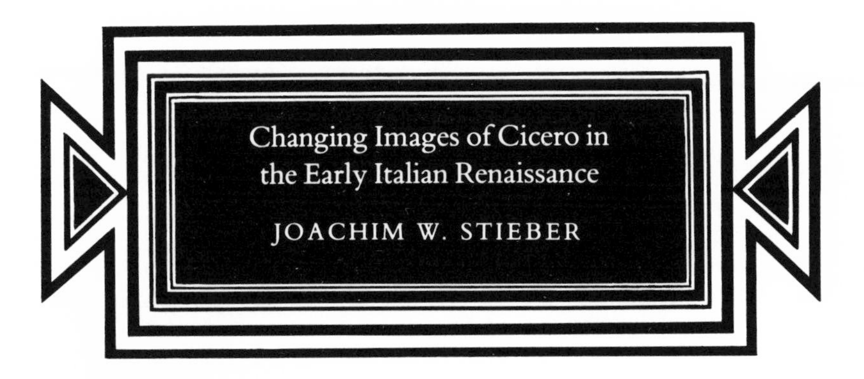

Changing Images of Cicero in the Early Italian Renaissance

JOACHIM W. STIEBER

TO SPEAK OF CICERO before an audience of the Alumnae College is to risk recalling memories—perhaps even painful memories—of translating his ever-so-long sentences in Latin class. It is regrettable that for many Cicero should have become in our day an author whose works survive primarily as school texts—difficult in style and apparently of little relevance to contemporary political concerns. This was not always the case, and I appreciate this opportunity to present Cicero in the context of the changing attitudes toward classical antiquity in the early Renaissance. Our discussion will focus not so much on Cicero's writings in themselves, but rather on how these writings were interpreted by Italian humanists and statesmen during the fourteenth and early fifteenth centuries.

Initially, we shall have to consider how Cicero, along with other great writers of classical antiquity, and pagan antiquity as a whole were regarded in the Middle Ages. We shall examine next how Petrarch ushered in the humanist movement in Italy by looking upon classical antiquity from a new perspective. Then, we shall see how the political circumstances of Florence, as a republican city-state, led its humanist statesmen in the early fifteenth century to adopt a view of politics akin to that of Cicero in antiquity. Indeed, we shall discover how ancient civic humanism came to be reborn in early-Renaissance Florence. By way of illustrating the historian's craft, I shall conclude by briefly indicating how the experience of our own history in the twentieth century has given contemporary historians a better insight into the appeal of Cicero's writings to Florentine humanists and statesmen in the early Quattrocento. My remarks are thus intended to contribute to the discussion of one of the themes of this Alumnae College, namely how classical antiquity, its survival and its revivals have continued to enrich Western civilization throughout its history.

Ever since the publication of Jacob Burckhardt's *The Civilization of the*

Renaissance in Italy, more than one hundred years ago,[1] it has been generally accepted that the Italian Renaissance was marked by at least some of the following characteristics: there occurred not only an increase in the knowledge of ancient Greek and Roman civilization, but classical antiquity came to be appreciated more fully on its own terms instead of being submitted to a Christian reinterpretation, as it had been during the preceding Middle Ages. Indeed, it seems quite plausible that the major revival of classical antiquity, which we call the Renaissance, should have begun in Italy. In no other area of western Europe were there so many physical reminders of the greatness of ancient civilization and no other people had as good a claim as the Italians to regard themselves as the direct heirs of the ancient Romans. We should therefore not be surprised that the Renaissance began in Italy. If we accept the year 410 as the traditional date for the end of the Roman Empire in Italy, we may, however, ask ourselves why should the Italians have waited until the fourteenth century, that is to say, for almost a thousand years, before embarking on a major effort to revive classical antiquity? In trying to answer this question, both political circumstances and economic factors will have to be considered.

In the century and a half between about 1310 and 1450 which saw the revival of classical antiquity, the Italian peninsula was relatively free from domination by the papacy and the emperors, the two great spiritual and political authorities of the Middle Ages. During this period, the papacy was at first in residence at Avignon and then, between 1378 and 1449, it was frequently weakened by schisms or by conflicts with general councils which challenged its supreme authority in the church. As for the German emperors who claimed to be also the rulers of Italy, it will be recalled that between 1250, the year of the death of Frederick II of the House of Hohenstaufen, and the reign of the Emperor Charles V in the sixteenth century, no German emperor was able, for any significant length of time, to impose his political authority on the Italian peninsula. In this political vacuum created by the absence, between about 1310 and

1. Original German edition published at Basel in 1860; English translation by S. G. C. Middlemore, with illustrations and notes: *The Civilization of the Renaissance in Italy*, Introduction by Benjamin Nelson and Charles Trinkaus, 2 volumes (New York: Harper & Row, 1958). The one hundredth anniversary of Burckhardt's book occasioned the publication of a number of commemorative studies, see in particular: *The Renaissance: A Reconsideration of the Theories and Interpretations of the Age*, Edited by Tinsley Hilton (Madison: The University of Wisconsin Press, 1961) and Hans Baron, "Burckhardt's *Civilization of the Renaissance* a Century after its Publication," in: *Renaissance News*, 13 (1960), pp. 207–222. Denys Hay, *The Italian Renaissance in its Historical Background* (Cambridge, England: Cambridge University Press, 1961) which appeared in a revised second edition in 1977, comments indirectly on Burckhardt's work and represents one of the best short modern introductions to the Italian Renaissance in English.

1450, of both a strong pope and a strong emperor, political power was exercised in Italy at the local level, either in independent city-republics or in city-states dominated by lords from the surrounding countryside. As Burckhardt suggested more than 100 years ago, and his argument has withstood well the test of subsequent scholarship, this temporary eclipse of imperial and papal authority in Italy encouraged a freer speculation about the nature of political organization. The writer who represents Italian Renaissance speculation about politics in its most fully developed form is, no doubt, Machiavelli.

The circumstances which favored the classical revival in Italy during the fourteenth century which we have mentioned so far, are: (1) the survival of many physical remains of antiquity, (2) the sense of being the direct heirs of antiquity, and (3) the relative freedom from political domination by the papacy and by the mediaeval emperors. We should now add a fourth and a fifth factor, both of them related to the material basis of the revival of ancient culture during the Italian Renaissance. On the one hand, we can say that by the mid-fourteenth century, sufficient material wealth had been accumulated in the Italian trading cities to sustain a cultural revival. On the other hand, the recurring devastation of Europe's population by bubonic plague for more than a century after 1348, not only reduced economic growth and with it opportunities for economic investment, but it also made men ever more inclined to look to the past before the advent of the bubonic plague, as a better age.

In order to appreciate the significance of the new attitude toward classical antiquity which led to the Italian Renaissance, and in order to understand how this attitude differed from the one which preceded it, we must briefly examine how classical antiquity was regarded in western Europe during the Middle Ages. Among mediaevalists, whether they be historians, theologians, or students of literature, any suggestion that classical antiquity was not really known in the period between about 410 and 1350, which is generally styled the Middle Ages, has been unanimously rejected. And rightly so. Indeed, how could one claim that classical antiquity did not survive in the Middle Ages when Latin was not only the language of the church, both for its liturgy and its administration, but also the only language of formal learning at the universities? Not only were the principal liberal arts taught in Latin, especially grammar, rhetoric, and logic, but also theology and canon as well as civil law. Our available time does not permit a detailed consideration of the fine arts in the Middle Ages and in the Renaissance, yet let me briefly point out that European mediaeval architecture in stone, whether in romanesque style or in its creative adaptation, in gothic are hardly conceivable, except as continuations and adaptations of Roman building techniques.

If in fact so many aspects of classical antiquity survived during the Middle Ages in some form, we must try to define how the survival and the revival of antiquity in the Italian Renaissance differed from that of the preceding centuries.[2] I have already suggested that the classical revival of antiquity which occurred in Italy between the middle of the fourteenth and the middle of the sixteenth century, differed from the survival of antiquity during the Middle Ages both in the *attitude* toward the classical past and in its *scope*. It was, above all, a change in *attitude* which led Italians of the Renaissance to seek more knowledge about ancient Greece and Rome. It is thus essential that we should try to understand this change in attitude which provided the driving force behind the major classical revival which we know as the Italian Renaissance.

The difference between a typical mediaeval and a typical Renaissance outlook on antiquity can be illustrated by referring to two Italians of the fourteenth century: Dante and Petrarch. As you may recall, only about one generation, in fact thirty-nine years, separated these two famous men of letters, both of whom were of Florentine ancestry. When Dante died in 1321 at the age of fifty-six, Petrarch was just reaching young manhood at the age of seventeen. And yet, in their attitude toward classical antiquity, we must regard the one as being typically mediaeval and the other as being the harbinger of the Renaissance. Let us begin with Dante's attitude toward antiquity which will exemplify for us the mediaeval outlook on the Greek and Roman past. Dante expressed his attitude toward antiquity, as well as his views on many other questions, in the *Divine Comedy*, his greatest work, which was written between 1311 and 1321.[3] You will recall that Dante portrayed himself in the *Divine Comedy* as embarking on a partly real and partly imaginary journey through Hell, Purgatory, and Paradise. What is of particular interest for our discussion is that Dante depicts himself as embarking on this journey assisted by a guide from antiquity, the Roman poet Vergil. Representing ancient poetic eloquence and ancient secular wisdom, Vergil guides Dante through Hell and even to Purgatory, up to the very garden of the Earthly Paradise. Yet at that point, Dante definitely takes leave of Vergil, his guide from classical antiquity. And it is Beatrice who will guide him during the final stage and end of his journey in Christian Paradise. Unfortunately, our available time does not permit us to accompany Dante extensively on his journey, but we should take note of

2. On the changing uses of classical models in the fine arts during the Middle Ages and the Renaissance, see the fundamental study by: Erwin Panofsky, *Renaissance and Renascences in Western Art* (Stockholm: 1960 and New York: Harper & Row, 1969).

3. Dante Alighieri, *The Divine Comedy*, [Italian text with facing English] translation and comment by John D. Sinclair, 3 volumes (New York: Oxford University Press, 1961).

the unmistakable message which his poem, taken as a whole, conveys to us. Ancient eloquence and ancient secular wisdom can guide the Christian for a stretch of his way, but they occupy no more than a subordinate role within a larger Christian view of man's destiny.

Dante's view of antiquity is also underlined in one of the scenes of his imaginary journey through Hell. Here, in the First Circle which he calls Limbo, the great poets, heroes and philosophers of antiquity are found. Although Dante regretted the necessity of doing so, he nevertheless placed such great men of antiquity as Homer, Ovid, Horace, Aristotle, Plato, Cicero, Seneca, and others, in Hell. Since most of them had lived well before the time of Christ or had, in any case, not been baptized as Christians, Dante had no choice, if he wished to include them in his poem, but to consign these great figures of antiquity to Hell. In doing so, Dante followed the traditional theology of his day, something that one might expect from a poet of his generally conservative outlook. On the other hand, since he evidently admired these great men of antiquity, Dante did not place them among the damned who suffer torment, but rather, in Limbo, a kind of antechamber of Hell which theologians had previously regarded as a region to which unbaptized infants would go after their death, not deserving everlasting punishment but nonetheless excluded from eternal bliss.[4] Dante correspondingly described the situation of the great men of antiquity in Limbo as one of indifference rather than of torment. They would, however, never be able to enjoy the bliss of the blessed and would remain enclosed, in their First Circle of Hell, by darkness. The only illumination which they enjoy is of an artificial kind, of the type given by the flame of a torch or other fire. True Light, as Dante knew, was reserved in traditional Christian theology, as an image referring to Christ. The pre-Christian world of antiquity, by contrast, was generally characterized as an age of darkness in which mankind was limited to the lesser brightness represented by human reason. As the Gospel according to St. John and also the Nicene Creed defined it, the "Light from Light," referred instead to the revealed truth of Christ.[5]

In the *Divine Comedy*, Dante thus reiterates the traditional mediaeval view of the great figures of antiquity by emphasizing that they belong to a past age of darkness which has been permanently superseded by the light of Christianity. The fact that Dante completes his imaginary

4. Fausto Montanari, "Limbo," in: *Enciclopedia Dantesca*, Direttore Umberto Bosco, Volume III (Roma: Istituto della Enciclopedia Italiana, 1971), pp. 651–654.

5. On the meanings associated with the term "Light" in the Bible, in the writings of the church fathers and during the Middle Ages, see the long entry "Lumière" in the: *Dictionnaire de Spiritualité, Ascétique et Mystique*, Volume IX (Paris: Beauchesne, 1976), coll. 1142–1183.

journey without Vergil when he ascends to Paradise, only underscores this point. Even on the level of literary language, we may note that Dante regarded Vergil only as an indirect model. Although Dante could write Latin without difficulty and did so on many occasions, he did not try to imitate Vergil by writing a major poem in Latin, but rather set out to write the *Divine Comedy* in his native Tuscan. As is well known, he did so with such grace and vigor that he helped to establish his native dialect as the definitive form of the modern Italian language. In his attitude toward classical antiquity, Dante thus shared the outlook of the mediaeval builders of the great Gothic cathedrals who did not hesitate to distort classical architectural forms like the column or the round arch in order to create a new style. It might be added that in his view of history and politics, Dante fully accepted, as part of the providential order, that the Roman Empire had become a Christian Empire ever since the reign of the Emperor Constantine the Great.[6] Moreover, Dante saw nothing incongruous in the fact that, ever since the reign of Charlemagne, the title of Roman Emperor had been borne in the West by Germanic kings.

As we turn to Petrarch, we meet someone who, by common consent, is regarded as the first man of letters of the Italian Renaissance. Petrarch's attitude toward antiquity represented a fundamental shift from that of Dante and of his mediaeval predecessors. Petrarch is best known today as the author of sonnets and of other lyric poetry in the Tuscan form of Italian.[7] Yet in his own day, Petrarch's reputation rested chiefly on his letters and on his poetic works in Latin. Petrarch's education and his social background distinguished him little from those members of mediaeval society who were familiar with the surviving aspects of ancient culture. The son of a notary, Petrarch was expected to follow in his father's footsteps. After receiving a sound education in the Latin language as part of his study of the liberal arts, he studied the civil, that is to say, Roman law, first at the University of Montpellier and then at the University of Bologna. Even though he appears to have been a good student of Roman law, Petrarch did not look forward to the idea of a legal career, and when his father died in 1326, he abandoned his legal studies. Using his small inheritance, he spent several years devoted to the writing of poetry in Italian and to the continuing study of Latin literature. Ever since an early age, Petrarch had learned to love the

6. On Dante's view of antiquity and history, see: Charles T. Davis, *Dante and the Idea of Rome* (Oxford, England: Oxford University Press, 1957) and A. C. Mastrobuono, *Essays on Dante's Philosophy of History* (Firenze: L. S. Olschki, 1979).

7. For an introduction to Petrarch's life and writings, see: Thomas G. Bergin, *Petrarch* (Boston: Twayne Publishers, 1970); Ernest H. Wilkins, *Life of Petrarch* (Chicago: The University of Chicago Press, 1961); Charles Trinkaus, *The Poet as Philosopher; Petrarch and the Formation of Renaissance Consciousness* (New Haven: Yale University Press, 1979).

eloquence of Roman writers such as Cicero. Having spent his paternal inheritance, he had to decide upon a career which would still permit him to devote as much time as possible to literary pursuits. His decision, made at the age of twenty-four, was to become a member of the clergy and he took minor orders in about 1328. During the remainder of his life, Petrarch was thus a cleric who lived from the income of ecclesiastical benefices for which he almost never fulfilled pastoral duties. In particular, during the years between 1330 and 1347, Petrarch was a chaplain in the household of Cardinal Giovanni Colonna, a member of the Roman aristocratic family. From his letters, we know that these years were filled with occasional diplomatic missions but that Petrarch also found time to pursue the study of Latin literature. The authors whose works he owned and which he most frequently quoted in his writings, were Cicero, Seneca, and Vergil.

Petrarch's patron, Cardinal Giovanni Colonna, usually resided at the papal court in Avignon but in 1337, and again in 1341, Petrarch was able to make the long journey from Avignon to Rome. The experience of his visits to the Eternal City appears to have had a decisive impact upon Petrarch. Indeed, it helped to define his attitude toward ancient Rome. One is tempted to think that Petrarch's residence at Avignon, as the son of a Florentine exile, particularly made him aware of Italy's great past, that is to say, of its ancient Roman heritage. At a time when most of his countrymen saw themselves only as citizens of a particular city-state, Petrarch, as an exile in Avignon, thought in terms of all of Italy and its common classical heritage. In his letters, Petrarch has left us reflections upon his visits to Rome which represent a fundamental shift from the mediaeval attitude toward antiquity. At Rome, Petrarch appears to have visited almost exclusively the architectural remains of ancient pagan Rome and to have paid only scant attention to the Eternal City's Christian shrines. During his visit he was, above all, struck by the grandeur of ancient imperial Rome within whose confines mediaeval Christian Rome appeared as small and puny. In Petrarch's mind, there had developed by the 1340's a clear distinction between ancient pagan Rome which he regarded as grand and magnificent, and mediaeval Christian Rome which appeared in a much less favorable light. Antiquity, as represented by imperial Rome, became set apart in his mind as a period of history which was distinctly in the past. In short, Petrarch came to see antiquity at a historical distance.[8] In subsequent letters, written in 1351 and 1359, Petrarch's outlook upon mediaeval Christian Rome, as opposed to

8. On Petrarch's view of antiquity and of history, see: Theodor E. Mommsen, "Petrarch's Conception of the 'Dark Ages'," in: *Speculum*, 17 (1942), pp. 226–242; reprinted in: Theodor E. Mommsen, *Medieval and Renaissance Studies*, Edited by Eugene F. Rice, Jr. (Ithaca: Cornell University Press, 1959), pp. 106–129.

ancient pagan Rome, becomes even more sharply defined. In these letters it is evident that he came to regard the reign of Constantine the Great, the first Christian Roman Emperor, as marking the beginning of a decline of "good literature," indeed, as the beginning of a period of darkness. By contrast, antiquity, which for Petrarch meant primarily Latin literature, came to be seen by him as a radiant age of "good literature." Even though Petrarch remained a devout Christian throughout his life, it is unmistakable that he had abandoned the traditional Christian perspective of regarding the triumph of Christianity in the Roman Empire as bringing about the advent of Light. Instead, he was struck by the fact that the reign of Constantine the Great seemed to usher in a long period of cultural decline, indeed the Dark Ages, as they were subsequently called. The contrast between Petrarch's outlook and that of Dante who had consigned the great figures of classical antiquity to an artificially illuminated circle of otherwise dark Hell, could not be greater.

Let us consider some of the consequences of Petrarch's new attitude toward classical antiquity. Seeing classical antiquity as an age whose cultural greatness had come to a distinct *end* at about the time of the Emperor Constantine, was the prerequisite for any wish or desire to revive and to restore ancient culture. Petrarch and his successors as Renaissance humanists never tired of emphasizing that an enormous gulf separated the spoken and written Latin of their own day (we would say mediaeval Latin) from the eloquent language of such writers as Cicero or Vergil. Fired with admiration for classical standards of eloquence, the humanists would systematically set out to gather the complete texts of ancient writers whom they now clearly distinguished from the authors of the Christian Middle Ages. Prompted by an historical vision of antiquity as a brilliant past age, humanists like Petrarch were at first primarily concerned with the restoration of classical literature. The desire to revive the culture of antiquity which began with Petrarch in the realm of Latin literature, soon came also to encompass an appreciation of ancient political thought, of ancient art and, eventually, also of ancient philosophy and mathematics.

We cannot here discuss all the successive stages and varied aspects of the revival of classical culture which, in their totality, we call the Italian Renaissance. Yet, it should be emphasized that the desire to restore the culture of antiquity had its origin in Petrarch's new historical perspective on ancient Rome and that the Italian Renaissance *did* begin with his desire to master the art of speaking and writing Latin in the manner of the ancients. In addition to providing his contemporaries with a persuasive rationale for restoring ancient culture as a whole, Petrarch also offered them a doctrine for the creative imitation of ancient pagan models. Even though this doctrine was not original with Petrarch, he gave it again such wide currency that it came to be a commonplace of Renaissance writers and artists. In view of the wide influence of this doctrine of creative imitation, it may be well to cite one of Petrarch's letters to his friend Giovanni Boccaccio in which he defined it as follows:

> A proper imitator should take care that what he writes resembles the original without reproducing it. The resemblance should not be that of a portrait to the sitter—in that case the closer the likeness the better—but it should be the resemblance of a son to his father. Therein is often a great divergence in particular features, but there is a certain suggestion, what our painters call an "air," most noticeable in the face and eyes, which makes the resemblance. As soon as we see the son, he recalls the father to us, although if we should measure every feature we should find them all different. But there is a mysterious something there that has this power.
>
> Thus we writers must look to it that with a basis of similarity there should be many dissimilarities . . . Thus we may use another man's conceptions and the color of his style, but not use his words . . . This is the substance of Seneca's counsel, and Horace before him, that we should write as the bees make sweetness, not storing up the pollen of the flowers but turning it into honey, thus making one thing of many various ones, but different and better.[9]

In this letter, Petrarch was using an image and even paraphrasing the very words not only of pagan authors like Seneca and Horace, but also of a Christian humanist and church father like Saint Basil the Great, the Bishop of Caesarea (ca. 330–379).[10] It was Petrarch's singular contribution to reintroduce and, by the force of his personality, to give wider currency in the Italy of his day to this concept of a creative imitation of classical antiquity.

Petrarch's enthusiasm for the study of ancient literature soon captured the imagination of his contemporaries. Within a few decades after

9. English translation of this letter, dated Pavia, October 28, 1366, in: Francesco Petrarca, *Letters from Petrarch*, Selected and translated by Morris Bishop (Bloomington: Indiana University Press, 1966), pp. 198–199.

10. On the parable of the bees as an illustration of creative imitation, see: Jürgen von Stackelberg, "Das Bienengleichnis; Ein Beitrag zur Geschichte der literarischen 'Imitatio'," in: *Romanische Forschungen*, 68 (1956), pp. 271–293. Saint Basil had evoked the image of the bees in defending the selective study of ancient pagan literature by Christians: Saint Basilius the Great, *The Letters*, IV, [Greek text] with an English translation by Roy Joseph Deferrari and Martin R. P. McGuire [= *The Loeb Classical Library*, 270] (Cambridge, Mass.: Harvard University Press, 1934), "Address to Young Men on Reading Greek Literature" (pp. 363–435, especially pp. 389–393). On the defense of classical pagan literature by Saint Basil and likeminded church fathers, see the brief and lucid introduction by: Werner Jaeger, *Early Christianity and Greek Paideia* (Cambridge, Mass.: Harvard University Press, 1961). For the history of the influence of Saint Basil's "Address to Young Men" ["Ad adolescentes"], see: Luzi Schucan, *Das Nachleben von Basilius Magnus "ad adolescentes"; Ein Beitrag zur Geschichte des christlichen Humanismus* [= *Travaux d'Humanisme et Renaissance*, 133] (Genève: Librairie Droz, 1973).

Petrarch's death, the teachers of rhetoric who taught ancient literature claimed that *their* discipline more than any other could enable man to realize the fullest potential of his humanity. Closely associated with the teaching and the study of rhetoric were grammar, poetry, history, and moral philosophy. This group of subjects was considered by those who taught them, and one might add, is still considered by those who teach them today, the "studia humanitatis" or the humanities. Italian students of the fifteenth century soon were to call a teacher of these subjects an "humanista" or humanist. The success of the humanist teachers of classical literature in promoting their particular subjects and in claiming for them the title of "the humanities" represented a shift within the liberal arts from logic to rhetoric.[11] Within the traditional trivium of grammar, rhetoric, and logic, the Renaissance humanists stressed the importance of rhetoric, whereas during the Middle Ages, the discipline of logic, enshrined in the so-called scholastic method, had been predominant. This shift from logic, the discipline which inculcated the proper use of reason, to rhetoric, the discipline concerned with the teaching of eloquence, can best be illustrated by contrasting the definition of man's highest humanity which was given in about 1270 by Thomas Aquinas, the greatest of the scholastic theologians, with that given in 1416 by Poggio Bracciolini, a humanist who later became chancellor of the Florentine republic. Whereas Thomas Aquinas had followed Aristotle in defining man as a "mortal rational animal" and therefore had regarded *reason* as man's noblest and most distinctive faculty,[12] Poggio Bracciolini defined *speech* as man's noblest character-

11. My characterization of the humanist movement as involving a shift from logic to rhetoric follows the views of Paul Oskar Kristeller. Even though many humanists placed a greater emphasis on man's dignity and on his achievements in this world than had been the case with mediaeval thinkers, this new outlook should be regarded as one of the *consequences* of their concern with ancient literature which constituted, in the last analysis, the primary and defining characteristic of the humanists. For an interpretation of the humanist movement in the Renaissance along these lines, see: Paul Oskar Kristeller, *Renaissance Thought: The Classic, Scholastic, and Humanist Strains* (New York: Harper & Row, 1961), reprinted with additional material as: *Renaissance Thought and its Sources* (New York: Columbia University Press, 1979).

12. For a listing of the numerous statements by St. Thomas Aquinas defining man as "a rational animal" possessing a body and a soul, see: Ludwig Schütz, *Thomas–Lexikon*, Zweite, sehr vergrösserte Auflage (Paderborn: 1895; reprinted: Stuttgart: Fr. Frommanns Verlag – Günther Holzboog, 1958), "homo– Mensch" (pp. 357–358). The Latin editions and English translations of the works cited by Schütz are listed in two recent biographies of St. Thomas: Ralph M. McInerny, *St. Thomas Aquinas* (Boston: Twayne Publishers, 1977), pp. 183–185, and James A. Weisheipl, *Friar Thomas d'Aquino; His Life, Thought, and Work* (New York: Doubleday, 1974), "A Brief Catalogue of Authentic Works" (pp. 355–405). Definitions of man as "a rational animal" possessing a body and soul or such statements as "man is man insofar as he is rational," may be found in the following readily

istic. Poggio expressed the concerns which were associated with the shift from logic to rhetoric in the curriculum of the schools during the Renaissance with great clarity and force:

For although nature, our common parent, gave to mankind intellect and reason as our chief guides for living well and happily, and none more excellent than these can be imagined, yet, I am not at all sure whether the power of speech might not be the most excellent gift of all that she has bestowed upon us, without which neither reason itself nor intellect would scarcely be of any avail. Speech, in giving external expression to the workings of the mind, is the one faculty which distinguishes us from other creatures. We should therefore consider ourselves under deep obligation to all those who have developed the liberal arts, but under deepest obligation to those who, by their patient and unremitting study, have handed down to us the rules of oratory and the norms of correct speech. For they have brought it about that in speech, through which mankind is chiefly distinguished from other living creatures, we should excel even other men.[13]

Two points may be particularly noted in this statement: first, Poggio regards man's rational faculties as "guides for living well and happily," and second, he singles out the faculty of speech as the noblest characteristic of man. Thus, the studies which enable a man to speak well and which make possible the *communication* of moral knowledge, rather than merely its *scholastic analysis*, came to be regarded as the noblest and most humane studies. Poggio Bracciolini's defense of rhetoric was written about forty years after Petrarch's death and it reminds us how influential Petrarch had been in his efforts to promote the study of the ancient classical literatures.

At this point, we shall turn to still another aspect of the revival of antiquity during the Italian Renaissance: the revival of an outlook on civic life which reflected not only the form of ancient literature and political thought but also its very spirit and substance. The rebirth of an ancient outlook on politics, and in particular, of the republican outlook

---

accessible English translations of Thomas' works: *Summa theologiae*, Part I: Question 29, 4th Article, Reply to Objection 2; *Summa contra gentiles*, Part III, Chapter 39, 1; *Quaestiones disputatae de potentia Dei* (*On the Power of God*), Question 8, Article 4, Objection 5 and Question 9, Article 2, Reply to Objection 10; *Quaestiones disputatae de virtutibus in communi* (*On the Virtues in General*), Article 12.

13. My revised translation of: Francesco Petrarca, *Petrarch's Letters to Classical Authors*, translated . . . by Mario E. Cosenza (Chicago: The University of Chicago Press, 1910), pp. 91–95. For the original Latin text and another translation, see: Poggio Bracciolini, *Epistolae*, Curante Thomas de Tonelli, Vol. 1 [= *Opera Omnia*, Riccardo Fubini, editor, III:1] (Florentiae: 1832; reprinted: Torino: Bottega d'Erasmo, 1964), pp. 25–29, and Poggio Bracciolini, *Two Renaissance Book Hunters; The Letters of Poggius Bracciolini to Nicolaus de Niccolis*, Translated and annotated by Phyllis W. G. Gordan (New York: Columbia University Press, 1974), pp. 193–196.

of Cicero, occurred in the political setting of early fifteenth-century Florence. Not only the general setting of Florence as a republican city-state, but very specific political circumstances provided a background that helped to bring about the revival of an attitude toward politics which was consciously modelled upon that of ancient Rome.

While it is well known today that the historical Cicero of antiquity had sought to perfect his skills as an orator and as a writer because he intended to use his rhetorical skills to further his political career, this was neither fully understood nor appreciated in the Middle Ages or even by Petrarch, the first humanist of the Italian Renaissance. Petrarch's admiration of Cicero as a writer was based not only on his orations but even more, on his philosophical works in prose. In these latter works, Cicero had set out to acquaint the Roman public of his day with Greek philosophy. In admiring particularly these works of Cicero, Petrarch followed the mainstream of the Christian mediaeval interpretation of the famous Roman orator and statesman. Petrarch and his mediaeval predecessors knew that Cicero had had an active political career and, that later in his life, after Caesar's advent to power, he had turned to the writing of philosophical works. Inasmuch as Cicero's *philosophical* works were broadly stoical in their outlook, glorifying devotion to public duties and praising friendship as well as the tranquillity of old age, they had been cherished by Christian clerics during the Middle Ages.[14] What had seemed so particularly plausible to these mediaeval students of Cicero, had been the proposition that the ancient orator, growing in wisdom as he grew in age, had turned from an active involvement in politics during his younger years, to the nobler calling of a philosopher in his old age. In short, mediaeval clerics warmly applauded Cicero's apparently voluntary withdrawal from active politics in favor of a more contemplative life as a writer of philosophical works. Such an interpretation must have been very appealing to Christian clerics who accepted St. Augustine's exhortation that Christians should fix their eyes primarily upon the City of God rather than upon the Earthly City.

Petrarch, who so greatly admired Cicero as a writer and who also preferred scholarly seclusion and the beauties of nature to the active bustle of city life, at first fully shared the prevailing mediaeval interpretation of Cicero. Like his mediaeval predecessors, Petrarch believed at first that Cicero had voluntarily foresaken active politics in his old age and had gladly turned to the writing of philosophy. Yet as Petrarch, in his determination to study as many manuscripts of Cicero's works as he

14. Hans Baron, "Cicero and the Roman Civic Spirit in the Middle Ages and Early Renaissance," in: *Bulletin of the John Rylands Library*, 22 (1938), pp. 72–97; reprinted with minor additions, in: Fredric L. Cheyette (ed.), *Lordship and Community in Medieval Europe, Selected Readings* (New York: Holt, Rinehart, and Winston, 1968), pp. 291–314.

could find, came upon the hitherto unknown letters which Cicero had written to his friend Atticus, Petrarch had to revise the traditional mediaeval interpretation of Cicero's motives. In these letters Cicero had expressed to his friend Atticus his keen regret over his exclusion from active political life. Petrarch was deeply disappointed to discover these, in his view, inappropriate sentiments on the part of the great Roman writer who, he felt, should have been glad to prefer philosophy to the active life of politics. Addressing Cicero in one of his works, where he engages in imaginary conversations with the great heroes of antiquity, Petrarch reproached the great Roman for his unbecoming sentiments.[15] Petrarch's reaction to his discovery of Cicero's true attitude toward politics is of considerable interest, for it reveals the limits of his ability to appreciate and to share an ancient political outlook. Cicero, the ancient statesman and writer, had indeed regarded leisure and philosophical study as justifiable only insofar as they could be regarded as a preparation for the subsequent participation in the public life of the commonwealth. For Petrarch on the other hand, and for most mediaeval clerics before him, the contemplative life had been seen as the highest pursuit of man. Petrarch's admiration of classical antiquity thus remained, in the final analysis, limited to its literary monuments and did not include an appreciation of the ancient Roman civic spirit. Petrarch rejected a life of action in the community and in the family but, at the same time, he did praise activity in the realm of restoring ancient literature and thus can properly be considered the first humanist of the Italian Renaissance.

The fuller return of the ancient Roman civic spirit in Renaissance Italy, did not occur in the secluded study of a scholar like Petrarch but rather in the setting of the republican city-state of Florence. As is often the case with important historical changes, the historian suddenly confronts them at a given point in time and then must attempt to construct a set of reasons, causes, or circumstances which can explain why these changes have taken place. In his interpretation of past events, the historian will necessarily be influenced by the circumstances of his own life and times. Let us then take leave of Petrarch, who died in 1374, and move forward in time to the period between about 1400 and 1440 and examine the attitude toward Cicero in the city of Florence. Here we find, in 1415, one of the city's leading men of letters, Leonardo Bruni, writing a biography of Cicero, deliberately called the *New Cicero*, in which he praised the fact that Cicero "in spite of intense preoccupation with his studies and his literary work, was capable of accomplishing

15. In a letter dated Verona, June 16, 1345. Cf. Francesco Petrarca, *Letters from Petrarch*, Selected and translated by Morris Bishop (Bloomington: Indiana University Press, 1966), pp. 206–207.

more practical work for the commonwealth than people unburdened with interests in literary matters."[16] For Bruni, Cicero served as an ancient model and example that involvement in the active life need not hinder but can even stimulate intellectual life. If we had only Leonardo Bruni's new biography of Cicero, on which to base our conception that there was, in early fifteenth-century Florence, a new outlook on the relation between the active civic life and intellectual pursuits, our argument would rest on a narrow foundation. We have, however, extensive evidence of a general shift in attitude. In the 1430's, the Florentine Matteo Palmieri wrote an adaptation of Cicero's *De Officiis* entitled *On the Civic Life* in which, making Dante his spokesman, he consciously praised the statesman who knows how to combine active involvement in the life of the city with literary pursuits.[17] In another work by Leonardo Bruni, his *Life of Dante* written in 1436, the great Florentine poet is praised in particular for having combined the life of a family man and citizen with the career of a writer.[18] In a similar vein, we may note that, during the 1430's and 1440's, in the funeral orations delivered on the occasion of the deaths of major public servants like the chancellors of the Florentine city-state, we find reiterated the theme that the lives of these men had fulfilled the highest ideal of the citizen by having combined intellectual careers as men of letters with active participation in the political life of their city. The political outlook of the historical Cicero had evidently achieved a rebirth, or, if you will, a renaissance in early fifteenth-century Florence.

How had this change come about since the time of Petrarch's death in 1374? Undoubtedly, a variety of causes and explanations will have to be considered and historians, being a cautious lot, usually prefer multi-faceted explanations. If you tend to look for economic explanations in history, there is relatively little in the economic history of Florence during this period which would help to explain why an active civic life should seem more praiseworthy during the 1420's or 1430's as against the 1370's. In terms of the structure of political life in Florence, the city had changed only superficially during this period. Both during the fourteenth century and still in the early fifteenth century, Florence can best be described as a republic whose political life was dominated by the upper middle classes.[19] If the mere existence of republican institutions

16. Cited and discussed, in: Baron, "Cicero and the Roman Civic Spirit," p. 21.

17. Baron, "Cicero and the Roman Civic Spirit," pp. 23–24.

18. Another aspect of the new attitude toward civic life was a greater willingness to regard the acquisition of material possessions as a socially acceptable pursuit. This has also been studied by Hans Baron, "Franciscan Poverty and Civic Wealth as Factors in the Rise of Humanistic Thought," in: *Speculum*, 13 (1938), pp. 1–37.

19. For an introduction to the political and social history of Florence in this period, see the following studies by Gene A. Brucker, *Renaissance Florence* (New York: John Wiley &

would have been sufficient to make possible a fuller appreciation of the civic outlook of the Cicero of antiquity, then such an outlook could have been fully shared and appreciated already in the lifetime of Petrarch, or even of Dante, when a republican form of government had been just as vital in Florence as it was in the early fifteenth century. On the other hand, if one believes not only in the power of ideas to bring about historical change but also in a certain autonomy of intellectual history, one might be willing to accept the notion that as the Florentine men of letters kept on reading more of Cicero's works, they eventually came both to understand and to share the great Roman orator's outlook on politics. This is an explanation which has much merit, yet it remains no more than a partial answer since it does not satisfactorily account for the extent of the change in political outlook which took place in Florence by the 1430's.

The rise of an ideology of civic humanism, modelled upon that of ancient Republican Rome, in early fifteenth-century Florence is a historical phenomenon that has particularly fascinated Renaissance historians since the 1920's. One may well ask why there has been such a strong interest during the last forty years in the rebirth of Cicero's political views in Renaissance Florence. As is so often the case, the interest in the past was prompted also in this instance by the concern with specific contemporary political issues. In particular, it reflected the concerns of one Renaissance historian, Hans Baron, whose scholarly career and interest in the civic humanism of early-Renaissance Florence illustrates how a historian's concern with the problems of his own age can sharpen (but we should add, sometimes also distort) the understanding of the past. Hans Baron was born and educated in Germany and spent his early academic career at the University of Berlin. Deprived of his teaching position in 1933 after the Nazis' coming to power, he left Germany and eventually settled in the United States where he has had a very influential academic career.[20] As a young historian in Germany during the 1920's, Baron was first drawn to the phenomenon of civic humanism in early Renaissance Florence since it represented something the *absence* of which he and one of his teachers, Ernst Troeltsch, keenly regretted in German society both before and after the First World War. Particularly in impe-

---

Sons, 1969) and, with particular attention to the ruling political elite of Florence in the period 1378–1430, *The Civic World of Early Renaissance Florence* (Princeton: Princeton University Press, 1977).

20. For a brief appreciation of Hans Baron's career and a bibliography of his writings, see the introductory essays by Denys Hay, August Buck, and Eugenio Garin, and the "Bibliography of the Writings of Hans Baron, 1924–1969," in: *Renaissance Studies in Honor of Hans Baron*, Edited by Anthony Molho and John A. Tedeschi (DeKalb: Northern Illinois University Press, 1971), pp. xi–lxxxvii.

rial Germany before the First World War, men of learning had all too frequently tried to avoid involvement in political life. As a student of early modern European history, Baron was therefore drawn to the study of the positive interaction between intellectual life and politics, both in sixteenth-century Calvinism and in the early Italian Renaissance.[21]

Firmly committed to the idea of seeking the origins of intellectual change in social and political circumstances rather than *only* on the level of intellectual history, Baron has argued that the origins of civic humanism in fifteenth-century Florence must be found in the successful resolution of a particular political crisis which the Florentine Republic had faced between the years 1400 and 1402. Let us briefly examine Hans Baron's argument.[22] In the last decades of the fourteenth century, the most powerful state in Italy was the Duchy of Milan which was ruled with a firm hand by Giangaleazzo Visconti between 1378 and 1402. Giangaleazzo had set out to extend his rule throughout northern and central Italy by creating a series of client states in which the traditional local administration would continue, but where the control of the military forces would be in the hands of a captain appointed by him. Giangaleazzo rarely worked through open conquest and preferred to achieve his ends through negotiation and political pressure. Particularly in the independent republican city-states, he tried to achieve his end by building up a local party of political supporters who would favor an alliance with Milan as the best guarantee of establishing a secure political order in Italy. In the last decade of the fourteenth century, the leaders of the Florentine republic watched Giangaleazzo's success with growing apprehension as many of their neighboring republics and traditional

21. Hans Baron explicitly pointed to his own intellectual links with Ernst Troeltsch in the preface to his first book: *Calvins Staatsanschauung und das Konfessionelle Zeitalter* [= *Historische Zeitschrift. Beiheft*, 1] (München: Oldenbourg, 1924), p. vi. In 1924 and 1925, Baron edited three volumes of the writings of Troeltsch after the latter's death in 1923.

22. Baron initially sketched out his thesis in two articles published in 1938 and 1939: "The Historical Background of the Florentine Renaissance," in: *History*, New Series: 22 (1938), pp. 315–327, especially, pp. 320–321, and "A Sociological Interpretation of the Italian Renaissance," in: *The South Atlantic Quarterly*, 38 (1939), pp. 427–448, especially, p. 441. Fifteen years later, Hans Baron presented his fully developed argument in: "A Struggle for Liberty in the Renaissance: Florence, Venice, and Milan in the Early Quattrocento," in: *The American Historical Review*, 58 (1953), pp. 265–289, 544–570. The latter article which contains the essence of Baron's argument was later included in the revised edition of Baron's major work: *The Crisis of the Early Italian Renaissance: Civic Humanism and Republican Liberty in an Age of Classicism and Tyranny*, Revised One-Volume Edition with an Epilogue (Princeton: Princeton University Press, 1966). The preceding work had first appeared under the same title in a two-volume edition (Princeton: 1955) which contained extensive scholarly references that were not included in the revised edition (1966).

rivals became part of the Visconti alliance system. During most of the fourteenth century, right up to the 1380's, Florentine foreign policy can be described as ideologically neutral.[23] At that time, it had been the aim of the Florentine leaders to increase their city's independence and to expand its territory in the surrounding countryside. This meant that the allies of Florence had frequently also been city-states ruled by lords, the so-called *signorie*.[24] In 1399, the Florentine political leaders found it necessary to change their approach when Giangaleazzo Visconti made overtures to the two independent republics of Pisa and Siena, suggesting that they enter into an alliance with him that would include the appointment of a Visconti partisan as captain of their military forces. Faced with the prospect that two of their closest neighbors and traditional political rivals would enter into the Milanese orbit, the Florentines became greatly alarmed and tried to dissuade Pisa and Siena from entering into a Visconti alliance. The Florentines reasoned, and this was the only argument they could offer since they themselves had frequently been at war with Pisa and Siena, that an alliance with Giangaleazzo Visconti was inconceivable for any republican city-state. In other words, they tried to represent their efforts to maintain their political independence vis-à-vis Giangaleazzo as a struggle between republican liberty and princely despotism. In the event, neither the Pisans not the Sienese were persuaded by the Florentine ideological arguments and accepted, in 1399, a Milanese alliance which included the appointment by Giangaleazzo Visconti of the captain of their military forces. To them, even though she was a republic, Florence appeared as a greater threat than their distant Milanese ally. And, one might add that they were right, since Pisa was to lose her independence completely after being conquered by Florence only a few years later (1406), and even Siena would come under Florentine rule in the following century (1555).

By the year 1400, Florence was thus surrounded by hostile city-states, most of whom were traditional enemies and who were now allied and guided by Giangaleazzo Visconti. In studying this precarious political situation of Florence during the years between 1400 and 1402, Hans

23. On Florentine foreign policy in this period, see: Nicolai Rubinstein, "Florence and the Despots, Some Aspects of Florentine Diplomacy in the Fourteenth Century," in: Royal Historical Society, London. *Transactions*, Fifth Series: 2 (1952), pp. 21–45.

24. The differences between city-states ruled by lords and those which remained nominally free communes were, however, not as great as has often been maintained. The government of a victorious political faction in a free commune was often far more harsh toward its political opponents than the *signoria* of a hereditary lord who usually ruled by controlling the traditional governmental bodies of a city, rather than by abolishing them outright. This problem has been analyzed in a convincing article by: Philip J. Jones, "Communes and Despots: The City State in Late-Medieval Italy," in: Royal Historical Society, London. *Transactions*, Fifth Series: 15 (1965), pp. 71–96.

Baron was struck by the fact that as the danger from Giangaleazzo Visconti increased, so did the Florentines' ideological identification of their city with the principle of republican liberty. The Florentine political leadership, consisting of men who had received a humanistic education, adopted such an ideological stance in order to encourage their fellow-citizens to make exceptional sacrifices and to strengthen their resolve to reject any accommodation with Giangaleazzo Visconti.[25] As it turned out, fortune smiled upon the Florentines and before the cautious and deliberate Giangaleazzo had fully tested the Florentine will to resist, he was carried off, in 1402, by the plague, leaving only an infant son as his heir. The careful system of alliances which Giangaleazzo had built up also disintegrated with his death. Enormously relieved, the Florentines were prompt to congratulate themselves after 1402 that they had indeed maintained their independence against the formidable threat of Visconti rule because they had so fully identified the cause of their independence with the ideology of republican liberty. Hans Baron has been able to show that not only Leonardo Bruni's new biography of Cicero, in which he praised Cicero's involvement in active politics, but also many other Florentine writings praising the active political life, all *postdate* the political crisis of Florence between 1400 and 1402.[26] In other words, he has been able to pinpoint more precisely both *when* and *why* many Florentines began to identify with and, indeed, to share the political outlook of Cicero in antiquity.

We may now ask why was Hans Baron able to date and to explain the revival of classical civic humanism in Florence even though the basic documents available to him had been accessible for more than one hundred years? For Hans Baron, the crucial starting point had been his original concern with the divorce of intellectual life and political life in his native Germany during the early twentieth century. His historical imagination was undoubtedly stimulated by his own position as a refugee from Nazi Germany, an experience which made him keenly

25. It has been convincingly demonstrated that the oligarchic leaders of Florence were not always guided in the period from 1382 to 1402 in their day-to-day conduct of foreign policy by the republican ideological stance adopted by the republic's chancellor, Coluccio Salutati, in his public statements. Cf. Peter Herde, "Politische Verhaltensweisen der Florentiner Oligarchie, 1382– 1402," in: *Geschichte und Verfassungsgefüge, . . . Frankfurter Festgabe für Walter Schlesinger* [= *Frankfurter Historische Abhandlungen*, 5] (Wiesbaden: Steiner, 1973), pp. 156–249. While Herde's argument modifies Baron's thesis with respect to the years before 1402, it does not detract from its value in explaining the subsequent political attitudes of a wider group of literate Florentine citizens in the early fifteenth century.

26. Hans Baron, *Humanistic and Political Literature in Florence and Venice at the Beginning of the Quattrocento; Studies in Criticism and Chronology* (Cambridge, Mass.: Harvard University Press, 1955).

aware of the meaning and the nature of the initial defeat of democratic regimes in Europe before the threats and then the onslaught of Hitler's Germany. In describing the political pressures which Giangaleazzo Visconti brought to bear on republican city-states when he tried to bring them under his hegemony, Hans Baron compared him with Napoleon and Hitler.[27] And might we not extend the analogy by characterizing those who accepted Giangaleazzo's blandishments as collaborators? It thus appears that the political experiences of his own life made it possible for Hans Baron to appreciate the importance, during the years between 1400 and 1402, of a civic leadership in Florence that had found in the commitment to republican principles a rallying cry for defending the independence of their city. Baron argues that Florence had in her humanist political leadership a moral resource which made possible a determined resistance against a foreign threat—the kind of determined resistance, as well as its absence, which Baron had observed in his own lifetime. We need only reflect upon the moral weakness of France in the years before her defeat in 1940 and compare it with the determined stand of Britain under Winston Churchill who offered firm counsel against compromise when the material odds which Britain was facing were no less formidable than those which other governments had failed to face. Hans Baron's contribution to our understanding of the revival of ancient political thought in fifteenth-century Florence thus reminds us that each generation of historians can make distinctive contributions to the understanding of the past, by applying the lessons of the present.

This survey could do no more than single out a few aspects of the changing attitudes toward classical antiquity during the early Italian Renaissance. We noted that Dante had not fully separated classical antiquity from other ages of the past and that, with many regrets, he had consigned the great men of antiquity to the artifically lighted First Circle within the darkness of Hell. Next, we observed how classical antiquity stood out for Petrarch as a distinct past age of great cultural achievements which he and succeeding generations of humanists wished to recover and to revive. In a brief excursion to early fifteenth-century Florence, we have seen, with the aid of Hans Baron, how the Florentine

27. Baron, "A Struggle for Liberty," pp. 284–285, and again, in: Baron, *The Crisis of the Early Italian Renaissance* (1966), p. 40: "In a like fashion, Napoleon and Hitler, poised on the coast of the English channel and made confident by their victories over every relevant power but one, waited for the propitious time for their final leap—until the historic moment had passed and unforseen developments had upset the apparently inevitable course of fate. This is the only perspective from which one can adequately reconstruct the crisis of the summer of 1402 and grasp its material and psychological significance for the political history of the Renaissance, and in particular for the growth of the Florentine civic spirit."

political crisis of the years between 1400 and 1402 can account for the revival in Florence of an outlook on politics very much akin to that of Cicero in classical antiquity. Not only classical antiquity itself but its survival and successive revivals can be absorbing objects of study which have continued to enrich the history of Western civilization. Undoubtedly, this is one of the reasons why we are gathered here for this session of the Alumnae College.

Suggestions for Further Reading

CHANGING IMAGES OF CICERO IN THE EARLY ITALIAN RENAISSANCE

Baron, Hans. *The Crisis of the Early Italian Renaissance: Civic Humanism and Republican Liberty in an Age of Classicism and Tyranny*. Revised edition. Princeton: Princeton University Press, 1966.

Bergin, Thomas G. *Petrarch*. Boston: Twayne Publishers, 1970.

Brucker, Gene A. *Renaissance Florence*. New York: Wiley, 1969.

Kristeller, Paul Oskar. *Renaissance Thought and its Sources*. New York: Columbia University Press, 1979.

——. *Eight Philosophers of the Italian Renaissance*. Stanford: Stanford University Press, 1964.

Panofsky, Erwin. *Renaissance and Renascences in Western Art*. Stockholm: 1960 and New York: Harper & Row, 1969.

Wilkins, Ernest H. *Life of Petrarch*. Chicago: University of Chicago Press, 1961.

PALLADIO AND ANTIQUITY

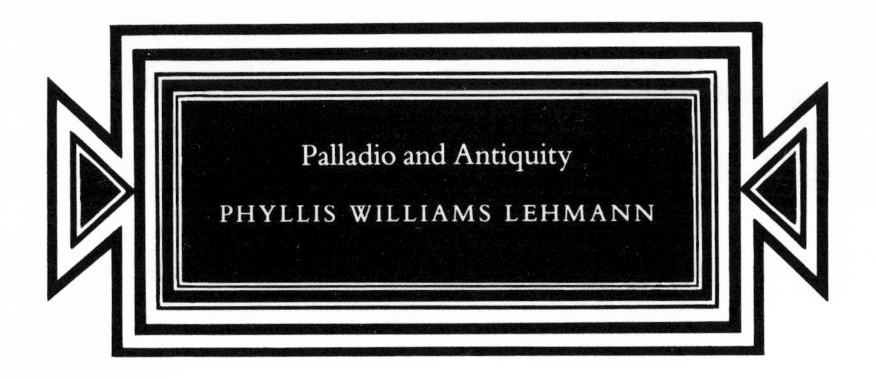

Palladio and Antiquity

PHYLLIS WILLIAMS LEHMANN

ANDREA DI PIETRO DELLA GONDOLA was born in Padua in 1508. Until the age of nearly thirty, he worked as a stone-carver in nearby Vicenza. Then he had the good fortune to be called to work on the Villa Cricoli, a villa owned by and designed by Count Giangiorgio Trissino, the most eminent humanist and intellectual of Vicenza. Writer, architect, and philologist, Trissino accepted into his household, as students, a number of young nobles. The Accademia Trissiniana, as the Villa Cricoli was later called, was a learned academy set in rural solitude, a Cinquecento version of the Platonic Academy in Florence. Trissino decided to include Andrea in this household and provided him with the name Palladio, a classical name alluding to Pallas Athena. It was clear that he could not provide an untutored stonemason with a well-rounded classical education or produce a "universal man," like the great Quattrocento architect and humanist Alberti, but he could help Andrea become a specialist. Hence he set Palladio to read on architecture, engineering, ancient topography, and military science—the fields in which he later became expert, not to say famous.

In 1541, Trissino took Palladio and two other students to Rome, where they stayed two years. It was the first of Palladio's several visits to Rome. Under Trissino's guidance, Palladio was exposed to the Roman Augustan writer on architecture, Vitruvius, whose ten books on architecture Palladio later emulated in his *Quattro Libri dell'Architettura*,[1] and to the monuments of Rome. The first fruits of this Roman visit were two guidebooks, one, *Le antichità di Roma*,[2] consisting of short descriptions of the classical ruins—till the eighteenth century, the prime guide for Rome. It was based on careful, measured drawings, witness those of the Porta Maggiore in Rome (Fig. 1), the Pantheon (Fig. 2) or his

1. *I Quattro Libri dell'Architettura* (Venice, 1570).
2. *Le antichità di Roma* (Rome, 1554).

restored plan of the Baths of Titus (Fig. 3)—part of a graphic survey of all the baths of Rome—or his reconstruction of the Forum of Nerva (Fig. 4) which, even in his time, had been sadly destroyed, as Du Pérac's engraving of 1575 shows (Fig. 5). Especially characteristic of Palladio's architectural drawing is his constant effort to present the ruins as complete buildings. Only a third of the gigantic Basilica Nova completed by Constantine was upright—the right aisle visible in Figures 6, 7. But Palladio made the building symmetrical (Fig. 8), adding a non-existent apse at the left—an example of his marked taste for architectural symmetry.

For Palladio, these years of recording Roman antiquities were a deeply moving, in a sense, religious experience. He regarded the "enormous ruins as a shining and sublime testimony of Roman excellence (*virtù*) and grandeur" and added that "the vestiges of so many of their sumptuous buildings . . . [give us] a certain knowledge of Roman virtue and greatness, which perhaps had not otherwise been believed."[3] As Wittkower has commented: "The practice of good architecture is for him a moral faculty, and architecture is one emanation of the unity of the sciences and arts which together consititute the ideal of *virtus*—a central doctrine of life and thought in the Trissinian Academy."[4]

Palladio was fascinated by bridges. His engraving of the Ponte d'Augusto at Rimini, which he considered the most beautiful of Roman bridges, shows its characteristic construction, including its typical spurred piers (Figs. 9, 10). The gabled niches he assumed contained statues. Such a substructure occurs in his project for the Rialto bridge in Venice (Fig. 11). He intended it to be both a bridge and a small shopping center. The shops which appear in both the ground plan and the elevation are normal Roman shops of a type familiar from Rome itself (Fig. 12). In his zeal to produce a monumental bridge worthy of a great city, he has not only added a temple façade or loggia, as he called it, at the center—a scheme that rather recalls the porch of the Pantheon—but has also flanked the entrances to the bridge by two fourway arches or gates that appear suspiciously like the Arch of the Gavii in Verona (Fig. 13), a city that he knew well and whose Roman antiquities he had recorded. Happily, this unfortunate mélange of Classical monuments was not built, and I expect that we all prefer the present Rialto. But this was a rare aberration on the part of an architect who, as we shall see, had a genius for absorbing Roman monuments and transmuting them into Renaissance buildings that have their own unity and integrity.

3. Rudolf Wittkower, *Architectural Principles in the Age of Humanism* (London, 1949), p. 57, quoted from the translation by Isaac Ware of the *Quattro Libri* in 1738.

4. *Ibid.*

Palladio's first public commission was to construct a two-story loggia around the Palazzo della Ragione, the great meeting hall of Vicenza's Council of the Four Hundred. Designed in 1546–1549, it has been known since Palladio's time as the Basilica. The plan of the vast, wooden-roofed Gothic hall appears in Figure 14. Palladio's structure, at the right, is a screen around the existing building (Fig. 15). The Basilica Palladiana is clearly modelled on Roman basilicas like the Basilica Julia and the Basilica Aemilia in the Forum Romanum (Fig. 16). The long flanks of the buildings are parallel to the Forum as the Palladian building is to the piazza in Vicenza. The general ground plans are related, and all three are essentially two-storied. Here, it is the general type of the building that has been emulated and revived. In Palladio's Basilica, we encounter the famous combination of the arch and lintel known as the Palladian motif: an arch supported by paired columns flanked by short, horizontal lintels (Fig. 17). Actually, the motif had been invented by Bramante, and Palladio seems to have observed it in Venice in Sansovino's Library on the Piazza San Marco (Fig. 18), which he had seen in 1548, in time to alter his earlier plans for the Basilica in Vicenza.

The commission of the Basilica brought a host of new commissions for palazzi and villas in Vicenza and the Veneto. I must confine myself to two: the Villa Rotonda outside Vicenza, traditionally dated 1550–1551[5] —and the villa at Maser, north of Venice, built for the brothers Barbaro from 1555 to 1559. The Villa Rotonda is not technically a villa, that is, an elaborate country residence for a gentleman farmer (Fig. 19). It was, as Ackerman has put it, a *Belvedere* for a retired Monsignore, who used it for parties.[6] Palladio comments: . . . "the site is one of the most agreeable and delightful that may be found, because it is on a hillock with gentle approaches, and is surrounded by other charming hills that give the effect of a huge theatre, and they are all cultivated. . . . And because it enjoys the most lovely views on all sides, some screened, others more distant, and others reaching the horizon, loggias were made on each face."[7]

Surely, this ground plan was not made for domestic life! Square, containing a central circle flanked by symmetrically organized rectangles in the four corners, it was approached by four loggias—or rather temple façades (Fig. 20). The sources of the Villa Rotonda seem to be complex and varied. One thinks immediately of the Pantheon (in spite of its different order), given the temple front, the attic story behind the porch,

5. Recently dated ca. 1566–1570 by Wolfgang Lotz in Ludwig H. Heydenreich and Wolfgang Lotz, *Architecture in Italy 1400–1600* (Baltimore: Penguin Books, Inc., 1974), pp. 314f., 393, n. 21.

6. James S. Ackerman, *Palladio's Villas* (Locust Valley, New York, 1967), p. 17.

7. *Quattro Libri*, II, p. 18. Quoted from Ackerman, *ibid.*

the dome, and its original steps (Fig. 21), and that Palladio, as we have seen, had made various measured drawings of the Pantheon. But seen from either the front or the sides, the porches project from the square block of the building (Fig. 22). This element recalls numismatic representations of the Temple of Concord in the Forum Romanum where, again, wings flank a temple façade at the top of a high flight of steps contained by die walls topped by statues (Fig. 23). From the side, Palladio's loggias contain conspicuous openings—as does the coin type. Yet another monument may lie in the background of the Villa. Palladio drew a temple at Clitunno, classical Clitumnus, not far from Trevi in Umbria (Fig. 24). It, too, has a related scheme

In the Villa Rotonda and in other of his villas, for example, Villa Malcontenta on the Brenta Canal, Palladio has grafted the temple façade onto the façade of country houses (Fig. 25). This characteristic feature, which he was the first architect to employ, shows his increasing application of Classical forms or building types to new purposes, his use of temple façades for domestic architecture—a free application of forms that has a modest forerunner in the Villa Medici at Poggio a Caiano by Giuliano da Sangallo (Fig. 26), where the extreme contrast between the temple-porch and the building proper is less bold and successful.

The Villa at Maser, however, is a genuine villa and analogous to the Roman villas that Palladio could have known from such Roman writers as Cato and Varro. Set in the midst of fields and orchards, its main unit juts forward, catching the light from three sides (Figs. 27, 28). It is flanked by long arcades in which farm equipment and animals were kept. Under the arches, there were dovecotes. The brothers Barbaro were Venetian aristocrats. Daniele, in particular, was one of the most outstanding personalities of the mid-sixteenth century. Mathematician, poet, philosopher, theologian, historian, diplomat, Aristotelian scholar, and editor of Vitruvius, his relationship to Palladio was a close and significant one.

The concept of a villa geared both for a humanist and a gentleman farmer was new to the Renaissance and reminds one of Cicero's half-a-dozen country houses scattered through Campania and Latium in the later Republic. Roman wall paintings of the Third and Fourth Styles, that is, of the first century A.D., reflect such villas (Fig. 29). Like Palladio's villas, they are characterized by symmetry, by a main central unit flanked by identical wings with prominent lateral terminations and often preceded by formal gardens. A second example (Fig. 30) shows a variation on the theme—a major unit—itself, in the form of a temple-front no less—is embedded in the center of a colonnade of projecting, horseshoe shape, again preceded by a formal garden. It has been suggested that some Renaissance villas were built on the ruins of Roman provincial villas. It is tempting to go further and to question whether Palladio knew such wall paintings—with temple-façades applied to domestic architecture—wall paintings found, let me emphasize, on the walls of Roman houses or villas.

A curious feature of the façade of the main unit at Maser is the broken pediment of the applied order into which a round-headed window rises (Fig. 31). On the flank of the triumphal arch in Orange, a monument that Palladio sketched during his visit to Provence, a related form occurs (Fig. 32). Alberti, too, whose writings and work Palladio knew and greatly admired, had used the motif even more literally in the façade of San Sebastiano at Mantua, which I show you in its present ill-restored state (Fig. 33) and, a second time, in its original form as reconstructed by Wittkower (Fig. 34).[8] Alberti, I expect, who had also been to Provence, must have picked up this unusual motif from the same arch. The motif is better visible in one of the sketches of Giuliano da Sangallo (Fig. 35). The *trompe l'oeil* decoration of the Villa by Tintoretto and the nympheum or fountain house containing sculptures by Alessandro Vittoria must have made Maser the most remarkable villa in contemporary north Italy.

Even more obviously rooted in Roman architecture is the Tempietto, the Chapel at Maser (Figs. 36, 37). Here, the Greek cross plan and the rotunda are fused and preceded by a Corinthian porch. The dependence of this miniature domed rotunda on the Pantheon is obvious (Fig. 21). It is fascinating to realize that the Tempietto anticipated a feature later added to the Pantheon and attributed to Bernini: the twin campanile that are identical in form with those at Maser (Fig. 38). The Tempietto was not published in the *Quattro Libri*, and its location in the Veneto was not easily accessible. But Wittkower, too, in a posthumously republished essay, assumed that the Tempietto was Bernini's source.[9] The double campanile on the Pantheon—now long removed—replaced the earlier mediaeval single bell-tower visible in this sixteenth-century drawing (Fig. 39).

A few final details are worth comment: the elaborate reliefs of the pediment, the statues on the die walls, and the swags linking the capitals. In his reconstruction of Roman temples, Palladio normally added such features—witness his engraving of the Temple of Castor and Pollux in Naples (Fig. 40). What was their source? In all probability coins. I bring back the earlier bronze coin of the Temple of Concord, which, if not identical in all respects, will suggest this likely source (Fig. 23).

Two further works should be mentioned at this point: Palladio's

8. *Op. cit.*, p. 45, fig. 7.
9. Rudolf Wittkower, *Palladio and English Palladianism* (London, 1974), p. 32.

illustrations for Barbaro's edition of Vitruvius published in 1556 (I show his reconstruction of the Roman house type, Figure 41, described by that not-very-lucidly-writing Roman architect) and the Teatro Olimpico at Vicenza, begun in 1580 and finished after Palladio's death that year by Scamozzi (Figs. 42, 43). This, the first theatre building since Antiquity, was based on Palladio's reconstruction of Vitruvius' difficult-to-understand description of a Roman theatre and, still more important, on his knowledge of the ruins of actual theatres in Verona, Pola, and Rome. A glance at the ground plan of the actual theatre designed by Palladio and a restored plan of the Theatre of Marcellus in Rome will prove the point (Fig. 44). Again, it is the type that has been revived as, a century earlier, Donatello had revived, on the basis of antique statuary, the first nude figure and the first large-scale equestrian rider known since late Antiquity. Indeed, it is amusing to note that clouds scud across the painted ceiling of the Teatro Olimpico, clearly an allusion to the fact that ancient theatres, whether Greek or Roman, were always out-of-doors.

Late in his life, Palladio designed two churches for Venice, San Giorgio Maggiore, begun in 1566, and Il Redentore, begun a decade later. San Giorgio Maggiore is attached to a large monastery on the Isola di San Giorgio at the end of the Giudecca—a magnificent location, whether one sees it in brilliant sunlight or suddenly emerging from dense fog as I did on a December day this past year (Fig. 45). Here Palladio coped with the age-old problem of church façades. He has solved it by what Wittkower has defined as the use of two interpenetrating or intersecting temple fronts,[10] one placed before and equal to the nave proper, its engaged order standing on pedestals, the other, slightly lower and to the rear, and equivalent to both the nave and the aisles and supported by double paired pilasters. This solution had been anticipated by Baldassare Peruzzi, in 1515, in his façade for the Old Cathedral at Carpi (Fig. 46). Here, too, a giant order has been used for the nave façade. But the lack of plasticity and contrast caused by the use of pilasters for both interpenetrating temple façades (as opposed to the powerful engaged main order of San Giorgio), the reiterated and distracting emphasis on semicircular arches in both temple fronts, and the loose, less tight interrelationship between the two ornamental façades is far less satisfying. The interior of San Giorgio, in both plan and spatial effect, has been strongly influenced by the bath buildings that had so powerfully impressed and interested Palladio during his Roman sojourns: the wide vaulted nave, the narrower aisles or niches, the massive piers embellished with engaged columns or pilasters (Figs. 47, 48).

Il Redentore was built by the Venetian Senate and delivered to the care of the Capuchin Order in fulfillment of a vow made on the deliverance

10. *Architectural Principles*, pp. 84ff.

of Venice from the devastating plague of 1575–1576 (Figs. 49, 50). The Doge and the Senators vowed to visit the Church annually in perpetuity, and instituted a cortège that passed over a temporary causeway thrown across the Giudecca Canal which terminated in prayers in the tribune or transept of the Church. Again, Palladio used the system of interpenetrating temple façades. Now, however, both pseudo-façades rise from the same level. The main temple façade is supported by a subtle and harmonious movement from the engaged order of the inner Corinthian columns to the outer Corinthian pilasters behind which, in lower relief, the pilasters of the secondary, wider temple façade stand. This tighter composition than that of San Giorgio is intensified by repetition of the main temple façade in the pediment, entablature, and engaged columns that frame the door of the Church. The complex symmetry of the façade reflects Palladio's conscious application of musical ratios. The proportions of a plan, an elevation, an interior space were conceived as visual harmonies and equated to musical harmonies and seemed to Palladio and other contemporaries to imply a universal Design. Hence the contemporary insistence on mathematics as a fundamental discipline.

The interior of Il Redentore is subdivided into three units: the nave and lateral chapels, the tribune or transept containing the altar, and the monastic choir lying beyond a semicircular screen through which light and sound could flow (Figs. 51, 52, 53). Palladio's study of Roman baths and his reconstruction of the Basilica Nova of Constantine with its symmetrical apses, its wide, vaulted nave and lateral niches or bays, its use of massive piers for actual support of the vaulting to which engaged orders are applied for decorative, ornamental, aesthetic reasons are at the root of this architectural-spatial experience. Even the screen of columns at the far end of the restored tepidarium or central hall of the Baths of Caracalla is echoed in the interior of Il Redentore in the columnar screen separating the tribune from the choir (Fig. 54).

Above the crossing or tribune hovers the splendid dome, a form dear to Roman architects. Although the illustrations may not suggest it, the quality of light reflects and reinforces the triple liturgical division of the Church: diffuse in the nave, ample in the tribune and the luminous dome, brilliant in the choir, where the blaze of light pouring in from the outer windows causes the hemicycle of columns to be silhouetted, and draws the worshipper and visitor toward the prime religious goal of the church—the altar and choir. Both these Venetian churches lack the rich sculptured decoration of the Tempietto at Maser. Chaste and pure, they are wholly unadorned either by sculpture or frescoes. Hence the powerful contrast between structural members and surfaces. The darker tonalities of the engaged orders and entablatures stand out sharply and crisply against the lighter surfaces of the walls and vaults, articulating their rich and contrasting spatial forms.

Personally, I find these supremely beautiful churches Palladio's most moving creations. Without his knowledge and use of the Classical orders, without his long study of Roman architecture, without his grasp of essential principles of Roman style, such buildings could not have been designed. A far cry from the uninspired and pedantic project for the Rialto bridge, they reflect the total absorption of an antique style and its transformation into a new style, a Renaissance style or, more precisely, a form of Mannerism that anticipates the Baroque.

Since the sixteenth century, Palladio's influence has been immense, not only in ecclesiastical architecture but in domestic architecture. A host of churches like Valadier's early nineteenth-century church of S.Rocco in Rome echoes the scheme of two intersecting temple façades (Fig. 55). But nowhere has the influence of Palladio been more pervasive than its effect on another humanist, the American humanist Thomas Jefferson.

Jefferson's political life prevented him from visiting Italy. Hence his knowledge of Roman monuments in Italy was largely dependent on Palladio's writings, especially the *Quattro Libri*, whose volumes dealt with the orders, domestic buildings, public buildings and town planning, and, lastly, with temples. In Jefferson's designs for the domestic buildings of the University of Virginia in the great quadrangle facing the Library, he tried to exhibit "chaste models of the orders of architecture taken from the finest remains of antiquity, and of specimens of the choicest samples of each order,"[11] (Fig. 56) and these examples he usually knew from Palladio. The Library itself, although modelled on the Pantheon, was in no way a slavish copy (Fig. 57). Halved in size, the columns of the portico reduced in number and altered in proportion, it was markedly changed by elevating the porch on a flight of steps, by converting the materials and colors of the Roman Pantheon into the rosy brick and white timber of America, by introducing windows in the rotunda given the purpose of the building and, above all, by carrying the white timber entablature around the brick rotunda, and thus linking porch and rotunda in a tight embrace in marked contrast with the loose, inorganic juxtaposition of porch and rotunda on the Roman temple.

Monticello is a villa with a temple façade and dome in Palladian fashion (Fig. 58). The interior of the house, Jefferson commented, "contains specimens of all the different orders except the composite which is not introduced. The Hall is Ionic, the dining room is in the

11. Karl Lehmann, *Thomas Jefferson American Humanist* (New York, 1947), p. 165, quoting a letter to Henry Tazewell written in November, 1825.

Doric, the parlor is in the Corinthian, and [the] dome in the Attic. . . . In the other rooms are introduced several different forms of these orders, all in the truest proportions according to Palladio."[12] To Jefferson as to Palladio, the antique orders had a special value. As Karl Lehmann has written: "The lawfulness and reasonableness of the antique orders, understandable in functional contrasts of vertical supports and horizontal weights, in mathematically defined proportions, were to both men the expression of a law of nature in architectural terms."[13]

Jefferson, like Palladio, had visited Provence, indeed Provence was the sole region in which he encountered tangible ancient buildings, and the encounter filled him with intense excitement. From southern France, Jefferson, the architect, wrote: "Roman taste, genius, and magnificence, excite ideas."[14] The same words apply to the still greater architect Palladio, whose excitement over Roman architecture enabled him to revive and transform it, to reconceive the ancient Roman heritage in contemporary Cinquecento terms.

SELECT BIBLIOGRAPHY

Andrea Palladio. *Le antichità di Roma*, Rome, 1554.
I Quattro Libri dell'Architettura, Venice, 1570.
Rudolf Wittkower. *Architectural Principles in the Age of Humanism*, 3rd ed., London, 1962, Part III.
James S. Ackerman. *Palladio*, Penguin Books, Inc., Baltimore, 1966.
——. *Palladio's Villas*, Locust Valley, New York, 1967.
Karl Lehmann. *Thomas Jefferson American Humanist*, New York, 1947.

12. *Ibid.*, pp. 168f.
13. *Ibid.*, p. 166.
14. Letter to Madame La Comtesse de Tesse written from Nîmes on March 20, 1787, quoted from *The Writings of Thomas Jefferson*, Definitive Edition by Andrew A. Lipscomb and Albert Ellery Bergh (Washington, D.C., 1905), vol. 6, p. 104.

FIG. 2. Palladio, *Quattro Libri*, IV, p. 81.

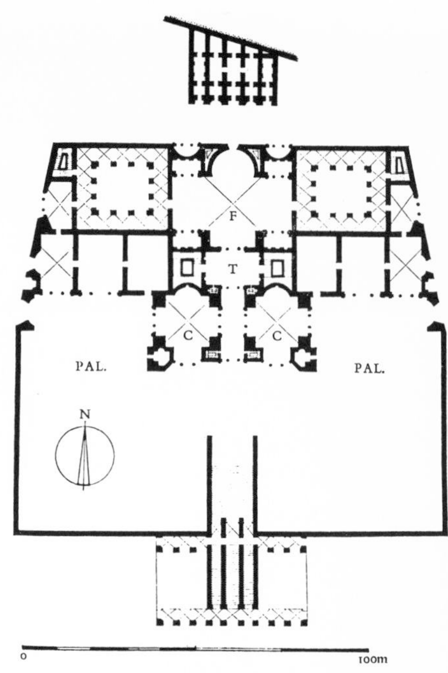

FIG. 3. Rome, Baths of Titus. Plan redrawn after O. B. Scamozzi, *Les thermes des romains dessinées par André Palladio* (Vincenza, 1797), pl. 5.

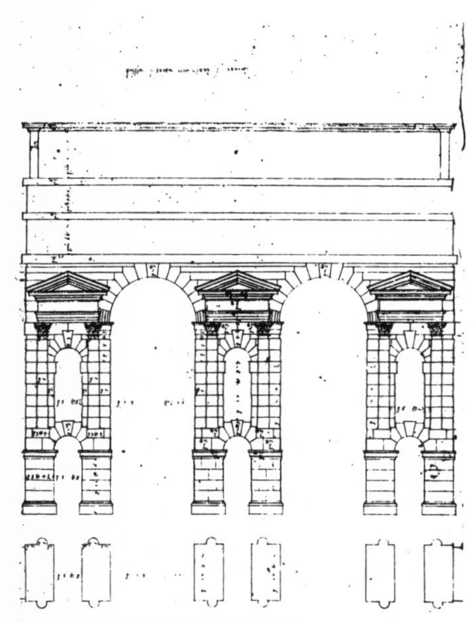

FIG. 1. Vincenza, Museo Civico. Palladio's drawing of the Porta Maggiore, Rome.

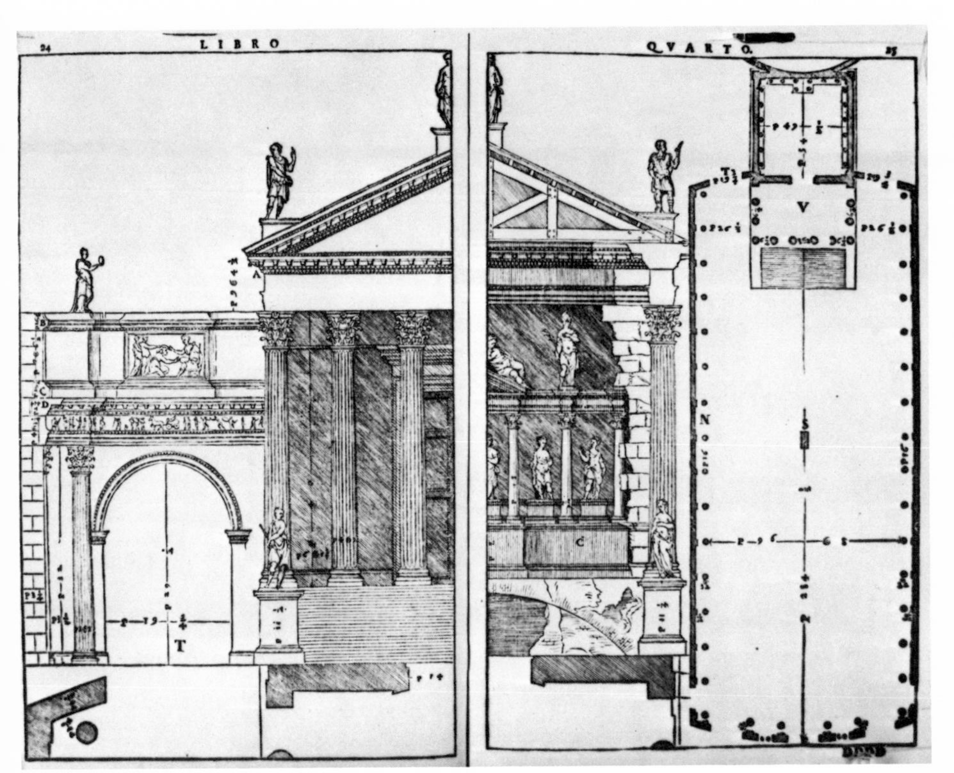

FIG. 4. Palladio, *Quattro Libri*, IV, pp. 24, 25.

FIG. 5. View of the Forum of Nerva and Temple of Minerva. Engraving by St. Du Pérac, *I vestigi dell'antichità di Roma* (Rome, 1575), fol. 6.

FIG. 7. Rome, Forum Romanum. View of the ruins of the Basilica Nova, completed by Constantine.

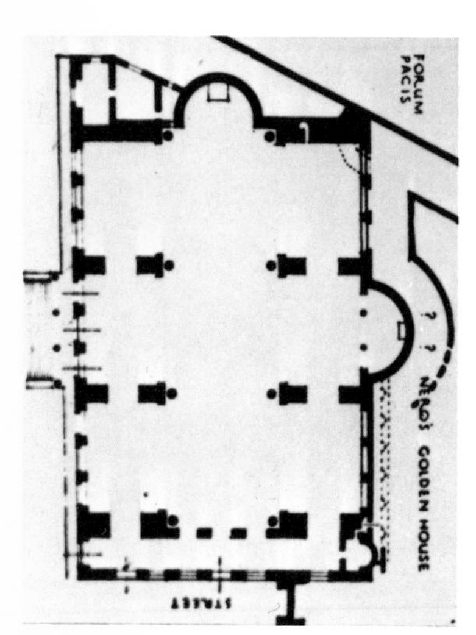

FIG. 6. Rome, Forum Romanum. Plan of the Basilica Nova completed by Constantine.

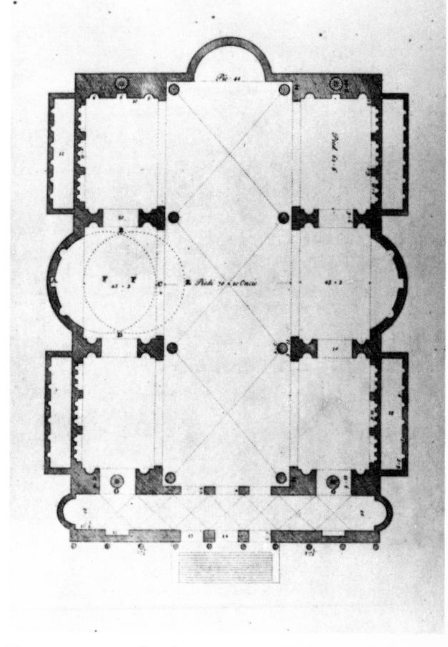

FIG. 8. Palladio, *Quattro Libri*, IV, p. 12.

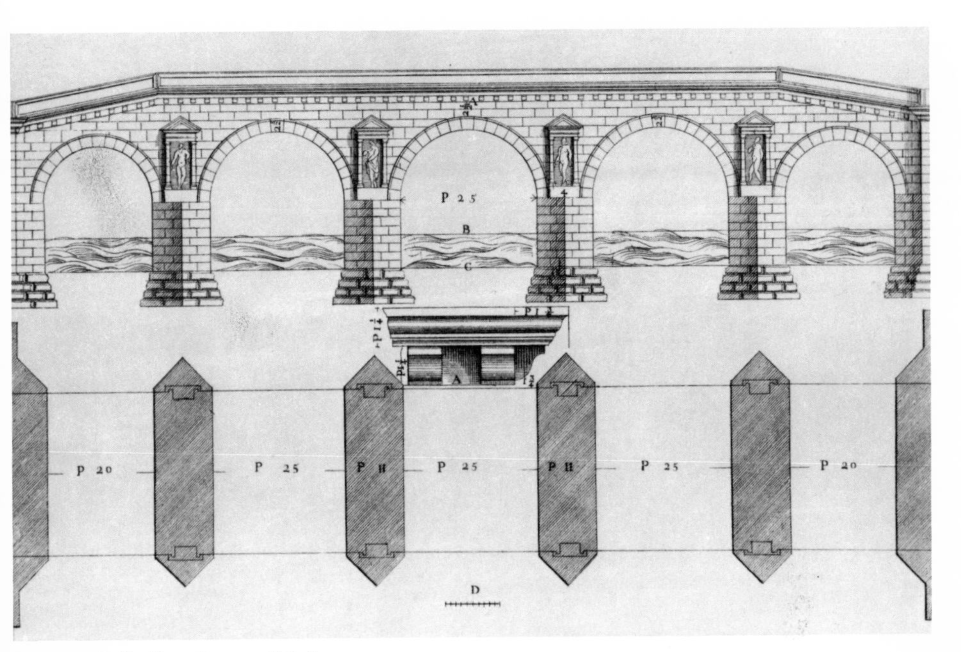

FIG. 9. Palladio, *Quattro Libri*, III, p. 23.

FIG. 10. Rimini. View of the Ponte d'Augusto.

FIG. 11. Palladio, *Quattro Libri*, III, pp. 26, 27.

FIG. 12. Rome, Forum of Trajan. View of the northeast exedra and shops.

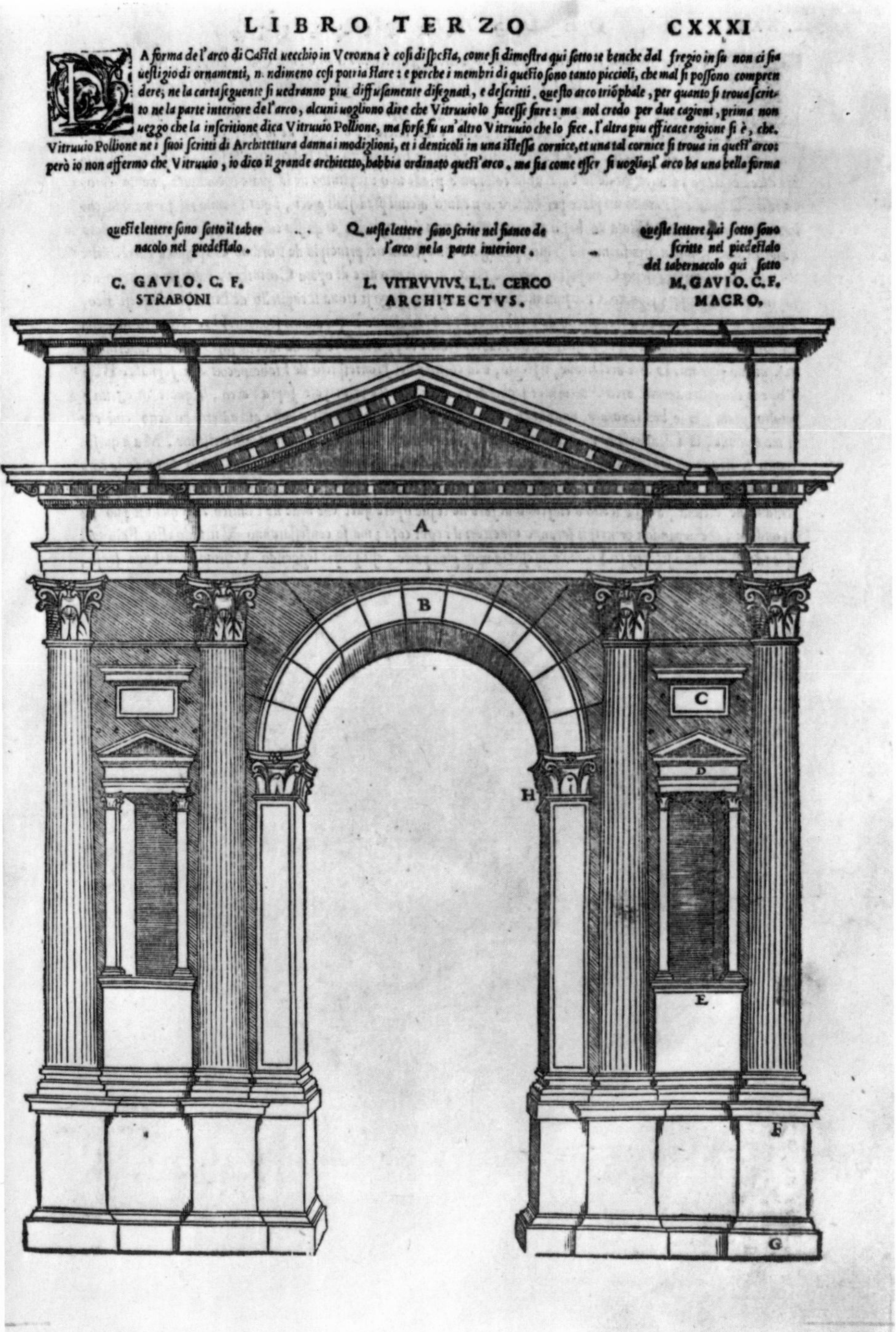

LIBRO TERZO CXXXI

LA forma de l'arco di Castel uecchio in Veronna è cosi disposta, come si dimostra qui sotto: e benche dal fregio in su non ci sia uestigio di ornamenti, nondimeno cosi potria stare: e perche i membri di questo sono tanto piccioli, che mal si possono comprendere; ne la carta seguente si uedranno piu diffusamente disegnati, e descritti. questo arco triõphale, per quanto si troua scritto ne la parte interiore de l'arco, alcuni uogliono dire che Vitruuio lo facesse fare: ma nol credo per due cagioni, prima non uezzo che la inscritione dica Vitruuio Pollione, ma forse fu un'altro Vitruuio che lo fece. l'altra piu efficace ragione si è, che Vitruuio Pollione ne i suoi scritti di Architettura danna i modiglioni, et i denticoli in una istessa cornice, et una tal cornice si troua in quest'arco: però io non affermo che Vitruuio, io dico il grande architetto, habbia ordinato quest'arco. ma sia come esser si uoglia; l'arco ha una bella forma

queste lettere sono sotto il tabernacolo nel piedestalo.

C. GAVIO. C. F.
STRABONI

Queste lettere sono scrite nel fianco de l'arco ne la parte interiore.

L. VITRVVIVS. L.L. CERCO
ARCHITECTVS.

queste lettere qui sotto sono scritte nel piedestalo del tabernacolo qui sotto

M. GAVIO. C. F.
MACRO.

FIG. 13. Engraving of the Arch of the Gavii in Verona by Sebastiano Serlio, *Il quinto libri d'architettura* (Venice, 1544–1559), III, p. 131.

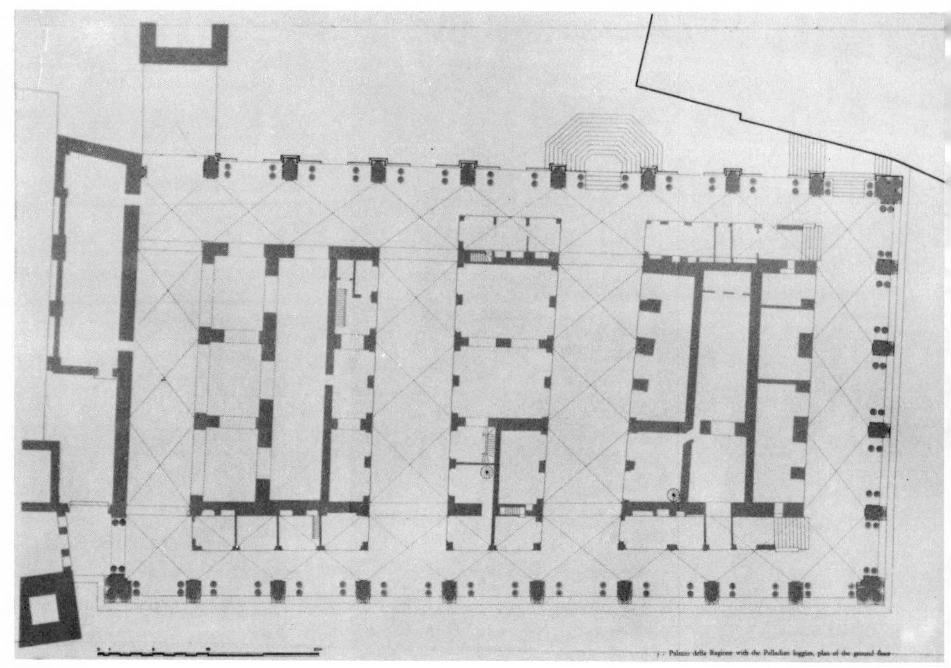

FIG. 14. Vicenza, Basilica Palladiana. Plan.

FIG. 15. Vicenza, Basilica Palladiana. View from the Piazza dei Signori.

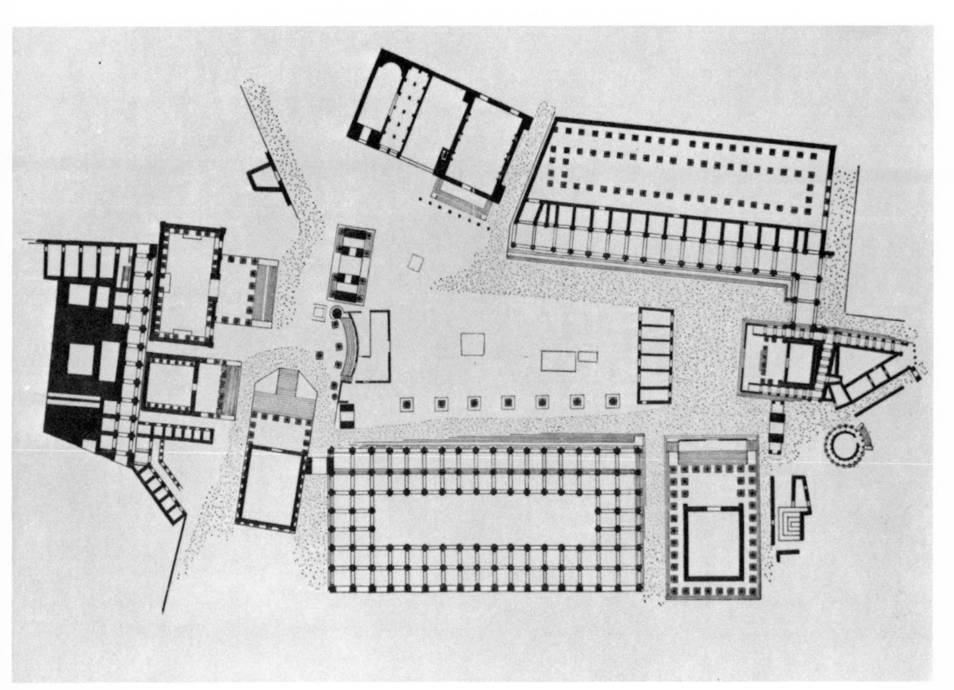

FIG. 16. Rome, Forum Romanum. Plan in the period of Constantine.

FIG. 17. Vicenza, Basilica Palladiana. Detail of the orders.

FIG. 18. Venice, Library of San Marco. View from the Piazzetta.

FIG. 19. Vicenza, Villa Rotonda. View of the exterior.

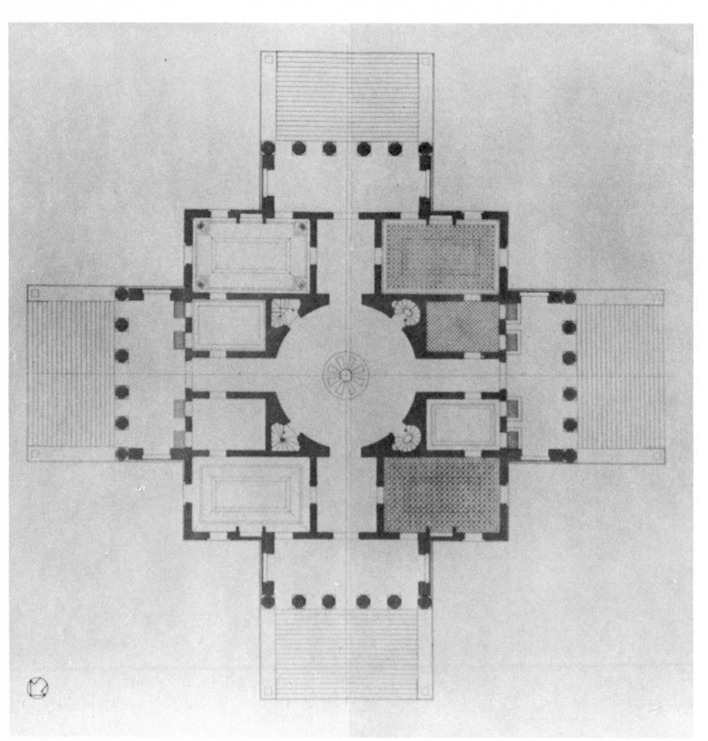

FIG. 20. Vicenza, V
Rotonda. Plan.

FIG. 21. Rome, The Pantheon. View of the façade.

FIG. 22. Vicenza, Villa Rotonda. Detail of the exterior.

FIG. 23. Reverse of bronze sestertius of Tiberius showing the Temple of Concord in the Forum Romanum (courtesy of the American Numismatic Society, New York).

FIG. 24. Giacomo Leoni, *The Architecture of A. Palladio* (London, 1715), IV, pls. LXXVI–VII.

FIG. 25. Malcontenta, Villa Foscari. View from the Brenta Canal.

FIG. 26. Poggio a Caiano, Villa Medici. View of the façade.

FIG. 27. Maser, Villa Barbaro. View of the exterior.

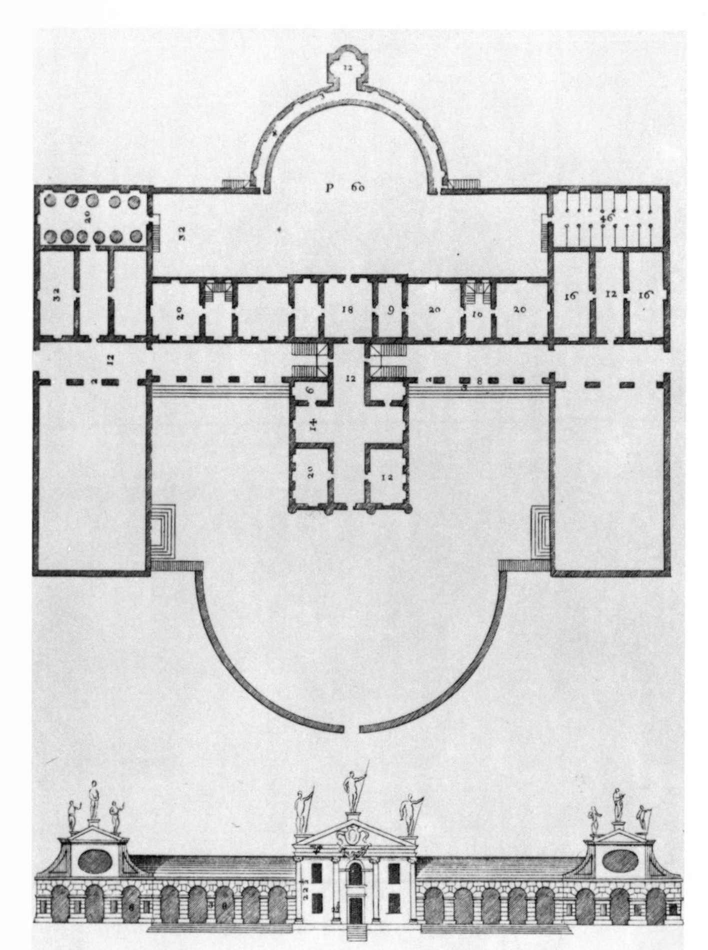

FIG. 28. Maser, Villa Barbaro. Plan (*Quattro Libri*, II, p. 5

FIG. 29. Naples, Museo Nazionale. Third Style wall painting.

FIG. 30. Pompeii, House of M. L. Fronto. Detail from the tablinum. Third Style wall painting.

FIG. 31. Maser, Villa Barbaro. Detail of the façade.

FIG. 32. London, Royal Institute of British Architects. Palladio's sketch of the Arch at Orange.

FIG. 33. Mantua, San Sebastiano. View of the restored façade.

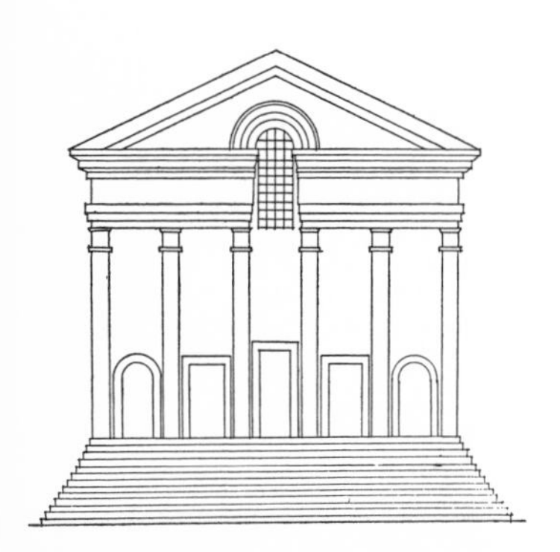

FIG. 34. Mantua, San Sebastiano. Wittkower's reconstruction of Alberti's project of 1460.

FIG. 35. Giuliano da Sangallo's drawing of the Arch at Orange (from Ch. Huelsen, *Il libro di Giuliano da Sangallo*, Codice Vaticano Barberiniano Latino 4425, Leipzig, 1910, fol. 25).

FIG. 36. Maser, Chapel. View of the façade.

FIG. 37. Maser, Chapel. Plan.

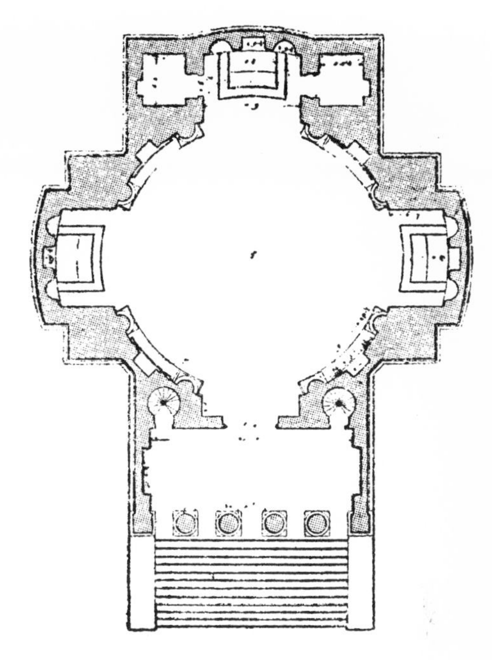

FIG. 38. Rome, The Pantheon. View showing Bernini's campanile of 1632.

FIG. 39. Rome, The Pantheon in 1534 (from Ch. Huelsen and H. Egger, *Die römischen Skizzenbücher von Marten van Heemskerck*, Berlin, 1913–1916, I, fol. 10r).

FIG. 40. Palladio, *Quattro Libri*, IV, p. 96.

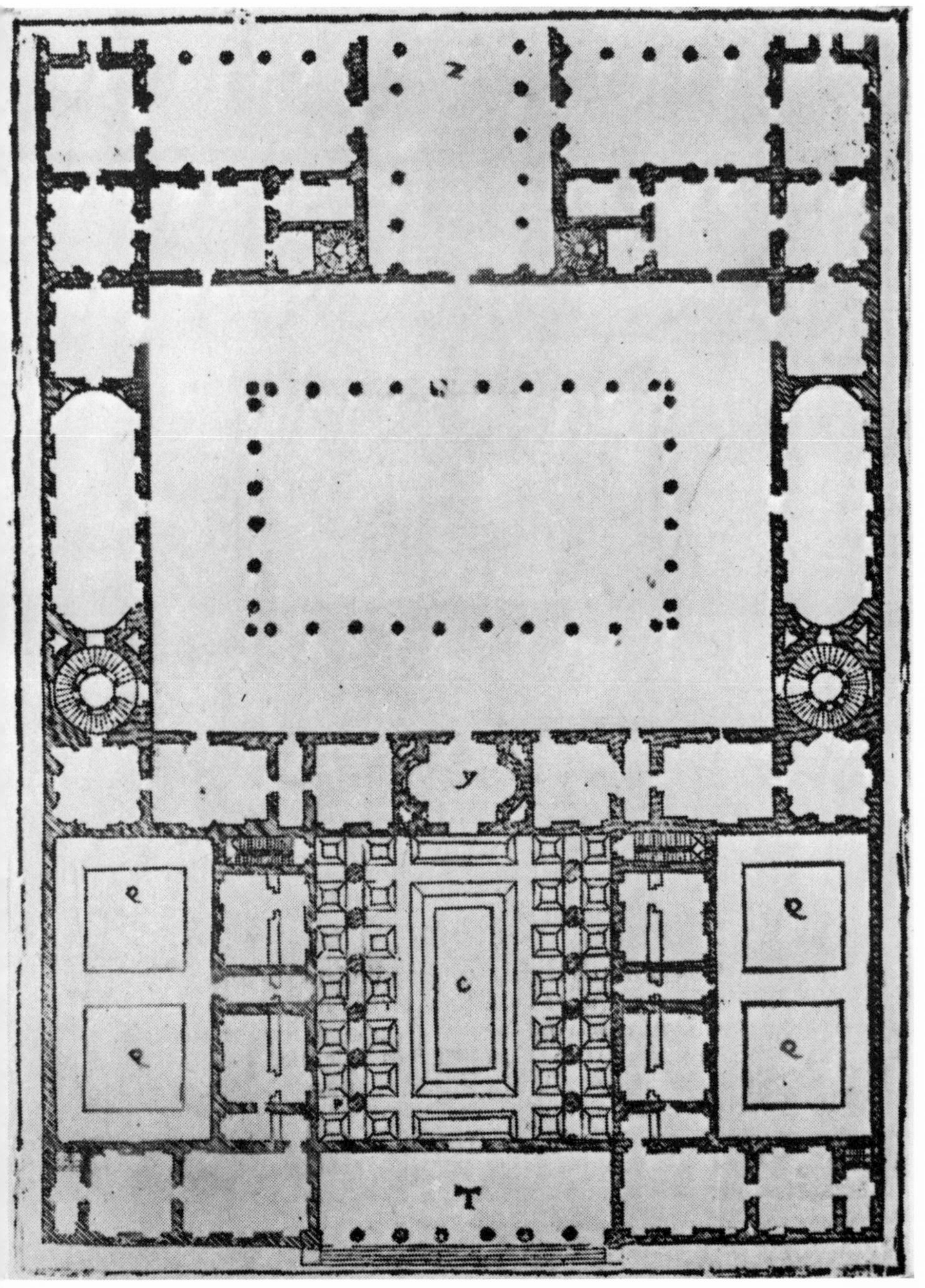

FIG. 41. Palladio's reconstruction of the Roman house type (from Daniele Barbaro, *I dieci libri dell'architettura di M. Vitruvio*, Venice, 1556, p. 280).

FIG. 42. Vicenza, Teatro Olimpico. View of the interior.

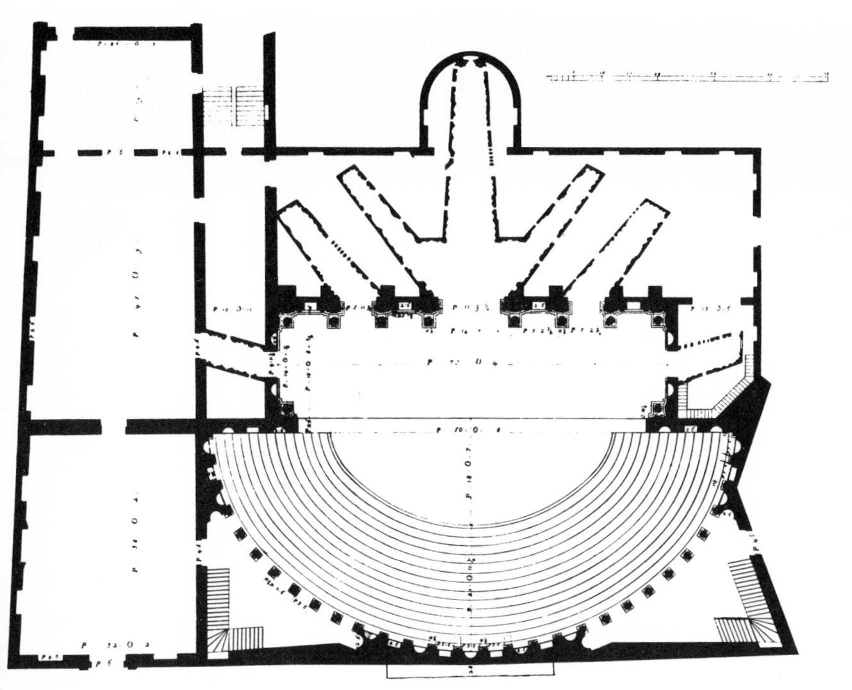

FIG. 43. Vicenza, Teatro Olimpico. Plan.

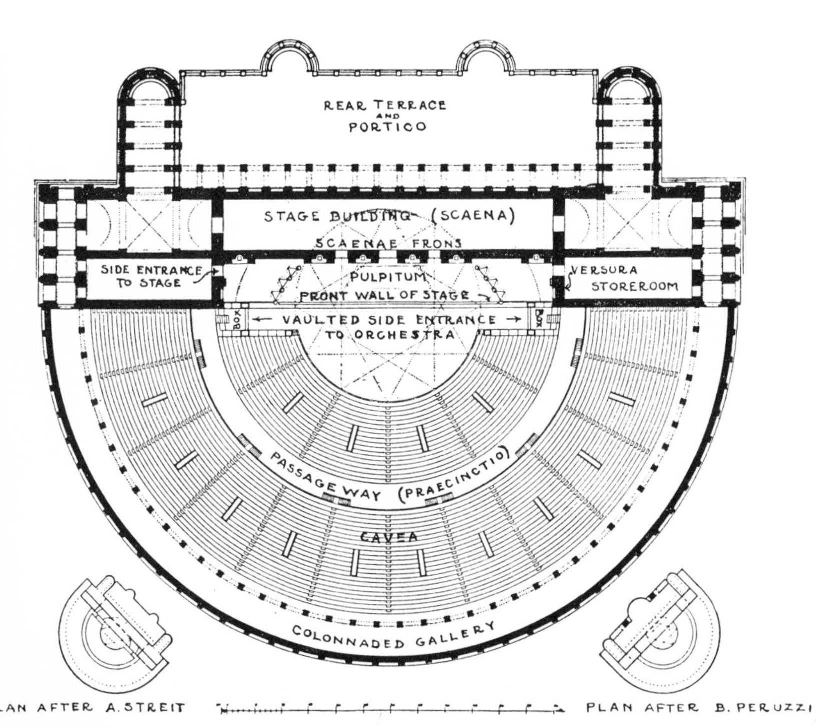

FIG. 44. Rome, Theatre of Marcellus. Plan.

FIG. 45. Venice, San Giorgio Maggiore. View of the façade.

Fig. 46. Carpi, Duomo. View of the façade.

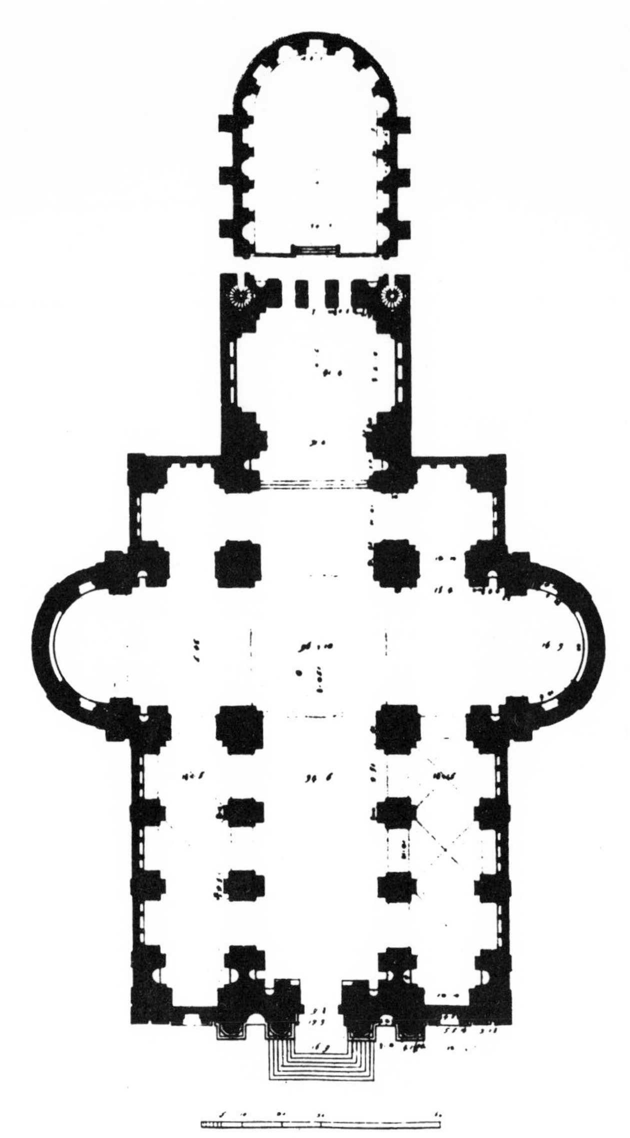

FIG. 47. Venice, San Giorgio Maggiore. Plan.

FIG. 48. Venice, San Giorgio Maggiore. View of the interior.

FIG. 49. Venice, Il Redentore. View of the façade.

FIG. 50. Venice, Il Redentore. Detail of the interior.

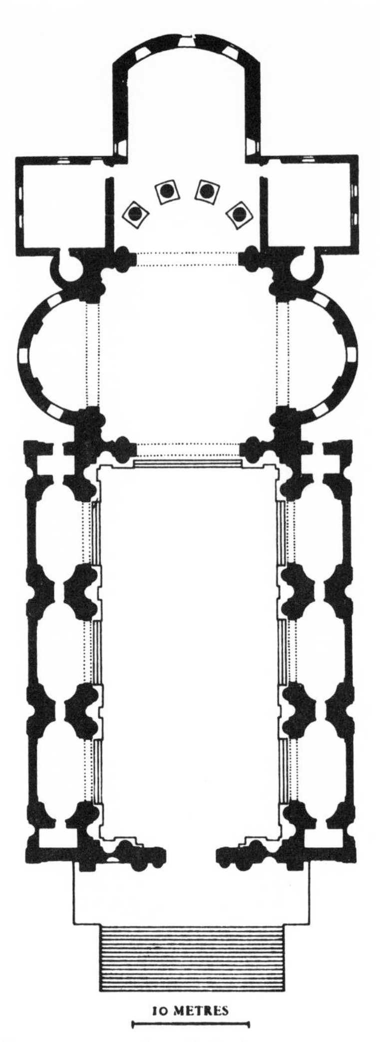

FIG. 51. Venice, Il Redentore. Plan.

FIG. 52. Venice, Il Redentore. View of the dome.

Fig. 54. Rome, Baths of Caracalla. Reconstruction of the tepidarium by Blouet.

Fig. 53. Venice, Il Redentore. View of the interior.

FIG. 55. Rome, San Rocco. View of the façade.

FIG. 56. Charlottesville, The University of Virginia. Aerial view of the east lawn gardens and Library.

FIG. 57. Charlottesville, The University of Virginia. View of the Library.

FIG. 58. Albemarle County, Virginia. View of Monticello.

THE LANDSCAPE OF ALLUSION: LITERARY THEMES IN THE GARDENS OF CLASSICAL ROME AND AUGUSTAN ENGLAND

The Landscape of Allusion: Literary Themes in the Gardens of Classical Rome and Augustan England*

JOHN PINTO

THE PAPER I WILL READ this afternoon is an outgrowth of research undertaken in collaboration with Professor Reuben A. Brower between 1973 and his untimely death in 1975. Reuben Brower was for many years a professor of English at Harvard and was an authority on English Augustan literature. During this period we were working together on a book entitled *The Augustan Myth*, which was to have been a collection of essays on the real or imagined analogy between the culture of Classical Rome and that of the so-called Augustan Age of England. Augustan literature is generally associated with the reign of Queen Anne (1702–1714) and with poets like Pope and Thomson whose themes and metrics were consciously modelled on the verse of their counterparts in Augustan Rome: in particular Virgil and Horace. A preoccupation with classical themes was by no means limited to the reign of Queen Anne; indeed it may be seen as a fixed point of artistic reference unifying English literature and the visual arts throughout the first half of the eighteenth century. Our central theme was to be the study of translation or imitation, especially "the dynamic process of assimilation," as Gombrich calls it, by which a writer or artist remakes in his own terms what he has lovingly learned in active commerce with masterpieces of the past.[1]

The Augustan myth offers unforgettable images such as the *Terra Mater* of Ara Pacis and *Augustus Imperator* with his outstretched arm—symbolic of the hero-prince who brought peace to the world, and who encouraged the revival of old Roman country life and virtues (Figs. 1 and 2). Our project was centered on the myth of the world that Augustus "created," a civilizing model and a set of ideal attitudes, given expression by poets, historians, and architectural theorists. The visual

* This paper was first presented to The English Institute on September 4, 1977.

1. E. H. Gombrich, "The Style All'Antica: Imitation and Assimilation," *Acts of the XX International Congress of the History of Art* (Princeton, 1963), II, 31. This sentence is adapted from R. A. Brower, "Visual and Verbal Translation of Myth: Neptune in Virgil, Rubens, Dryden," *Daedalus*, 1972 (Winter), p.157.

focus of the book was to be Rome, vividly present to us as to the English Augustans in temples, arches, forums, palaces, and villas.

In any venture such as this, which deals with relations between works produced in different media and within very different cultures, there is always a temptation to indulge in fanciful analogies. While mindful of this danger, we were still more wary of formulating a rigid thesis which would do violence to the rich variety and subtle relationships in the texts we chose to study. The true aim of our method was rather to explore honestly parallel expressions of certain ideals of art and social life—"parallel," as Pope said of his *Homer*, "tho' not the same."[2] I will concentrate today on several visual expressions of the Augustan myth, tracing the way in which the art and literature of Classical Antiquity, as interpreted or transmitted directly through the Renaissance, came to exert a powerful influence on the English Augustans.

The poetry and design of landscape, which constitute one of the most significant artistic achievements of the two Augustan ages, will be the focal point of my examination. Certain landscape themes—indeed specific buildings, statues, and gardens—called to mind myths and literary traditions which transcended their obvious outward forms and made them powerful and compelling metaphors. To take one or two examples at random: a poetic epistle describing one's life in the country suggested a return to Golden Age simplicities; to make an artificial stream was to create a Euripus or Styx; to open up a valley was to make another Tempe; to speak of Maecenas was to evoke the image of a beneficent patron. Like Pliny, who restored the Temple of Ceres on his Tuscan property, Lord Arlington, the protégé of Charles II, built a new church in Eusten Park at John Evelyn's suggestion. Not a world-shaking achievement, and one motivated by a mixture of piety and pride—but thanks to such men the country world of ancient Italy and modern England was the richer. How the eye and mind ache in twentieth-century landscapes for buildings which in their style and historical associations allude to values other than economic.

Today I propose to look at some of the mythological, topographical, and historical allusions which played such a prominent role in the landscapes of Augustan Rome and eighteenth-century England. The sacred or sacral-idyllic landscape has a long literary and artistic tradition which can be traced back at least as far as Homer. Such landscapes are not mere descriptions or representations of specific places, though they may allude to them, but rather are symbolic idealizations, in which divine and human forms play the primary role. Nature is presented in its divine aspects, as the setting for human activity. This can clearly be seen

2. *Iliad*, XIII, n. XXXIX, v. 721.

in a Pompeian fresco of about 70 B.C., representing Paris on Mount Ida (Fig. 3). At first glance the painting would appear to represent a simple shepherd resting under the shade of a tree while tending his flocks. It is only upon closer inspection, when we notice the statue of Priapus in the middleground and the rustic shrine enclosing the tree, that the scene takes on a religious significance. Closer study reveals the shepherd's Phrygian cap, identifying him as Paris, and thus a mythical association is imparted to the picture as well. Finally, we notice the reclining figure in the background, a personification of Mount Ida, whose presence identifies the rugged peak dominating the landscape and further enhances our appreciation of the divine in nature. As the direct result of these allusions, this wall painting becomes much more than a straightforward landscape view, and is enriched by multiple levels of religious, mythical, and topographical association.

While Roman landscape paintings of this kind became well known only after 1750, following the discovery of Pompeii, other aids to Renaissance humanists and English Augustans in the visual reconstruction of passages from Virgil and Ovid lay close at hand. The landscape of the Italian countryside, and particularly that of the Campagna surrounding Rome, was a source of inspiration to which the English Augustans had frequent recourse. The crucial role played by seventeenth-century painters such as Poussin and Claude Lorraine in making available portable distillations of this classical scenery is well known. To a significant degree, however, scholarly preoccupation with documenting the presence of specific painted views in the collections of English gardeners has tended to obscure the equally powerful influence of the actual landscape, as studied by generations of English travellers on the Grand Tour. Perhaps the most famous survival of a Roman sacred landscape is the so-called Temple of Sibyl at Tivoli (Fig. 4), which was appreciated as much for its natural beauty as for the way in which it so superbly combines many of the elements of the sacred landscape as described by classical poets, in particular, Ovid.

The first words of Ovid's tale of Daphne point ahead to his picture of the most romantic of ancient paradises, the Vale of Tempe: "Phoebus' first love was Daphne, daughter of Peneus, the river god of Thessaly."[3] (It is this part of the *Metamorphoses*, of course, that Pope recast in the Lodona section of "Windsor Forest," substituting the River Thames for the Peneus.) During the story of Apollo's pursuit, there are brief glimpses of the dark and frightening Ovidian wilderness: "She fled even the name of love, in the deep hiding places of the woods," and "she roamed through the pathless forests." Seeking her father's river close

3. Ovid, *Metamorphoses*, I, 459.

by, Daphne prayed for help and at once began to feel the terrifying and grotesque change that Bernini rendered so masterfully. Ovid pictures the place where Daphne's father lives in imagery recalling similar sorts of Italian landscape, natural and man-made:

There is a vale in Thessaly which steep-wooded slopes surround on every side. Men call it Tempe. Through this the river Peneus flows from the foot of Pindus with foam-flecked waters and by its heavy fall forms clouds which drive along fine, smoke-like mist, sprinkles the tops of trees with spray, and deafens even remoter regions by its roar. Here is the home, the seat, the inmost haunt of the mighty stream. Here, seated in a cave made from the overhanging crag, he was giving laws to his waters and to his water nymphs.[4]

Whether or not, as Grimal supposes, this scene reflects the valley in Tivoli where the falls of the Anio still toss up their smoking clouds of mist and sprinkle the tree tops, it is certain that the lines show Ovid's familiarity with the language of garden architects: *nemus*, the carefully composed grove of a landscaper, in contrast with *silva*, the wild woods; the *domus*, the house of the god; *sedes*, his country seat; *antro*, the cave which betrays its grotto-like form by the phrase "made from the overhanging crag," and by the statue-like pose of the god so visibly seated in the presence of the nymphs.[5] It is almost impossible not to see a Roman nymphaeum with the rough masonry of its vault, its gods and fountains. But the scene is more than a piece of garden décor; it is a shrine of the nymphs in a magnificent landscape, the Vale of Tempe, one of the classic motifs of Roman gardening on a large scale, as we will shortly see in the "Tempe" of Hadrian's Villa.

While Pliny the Younger cannot strictly be considered a Roman Augustan (he lived a full century after the reign of Augustus), his letters give us a picture of another sacred landscape surviving in many of its essentials, which was already in existence by the end of the Republic: the springs of Clitumnus, near Spoleto. Pliny was a successful lawyer and an able administrator under the emperor Trajan; and throughout his life he continued to be both man of affairs and a man of letters. He was an active and beneficent citizen of his native town of Como, and a good manager of his numerous country estates. In combining these various lives effectively and gracefully, Pliny seems to anticipate perfectly the English Augustan type, government official or banker, shuttling between London and his country house in Surrey or Wiltshire, adept at writing a speech or a letter in prose or verse, able to produce an apt quotation from Virgil or Horace, and like his Roman counterpart, a

4. *Ibid.*, I, 568–576 (F. J. Miller, trans., Cambridge, 1951, I, 43).

5. P. Grimal, *Les jardins romains* (second edition), Paris, 1969, p. 406. Since 1834 the falls of the Anio have been diverted to the far side of the valley opposite the Temple of Sibyl.

builder, a planter, and a farm manager. Pliny's description of Clitumnus corresponds closely to the site as we see it today, although the temple is probably a pastiche of the eighth century[6] (Fig. 5):

> At the foot of a little hill, covered with venerable and shady cypress trees, the river . . . forms a broad pool so clear and glassy that you may count the shining pebbles and the little pieces of money which are thrown into it. . . . The banks are thickly clad with ash and poplar trees, whose verdant reflections are as distinctly seen in the translucent stream as if they were actually sunk in it. . . . Near it is a primitive and holy temple, wherein stands the river god Clitumnus clothed in a purple-bordered robe. . . . Several little chapels are scattered round, each containing the statue of a different god. . . . there are several other lesser streams which . . . lose themselves into the river; over which a bridge is built, . . . and villas, wherever the river is most beautiful, are situated upon its banks.[7]

The close correspondence of a well-known site and a classical literary passage is of interest, but of special significance is the extent to which both anticipate so completely the English landscape gardens of the eighteenth century. Furthermore, we see anticipations not just of form, but of the sacred presence which animates this landscape, trees and man-made structures alike.

The so-called Triopion, or estate of Herodius Atticus off the Via Appia near Rome, offers one final example of a surviving sacred landscape (Fig. 6). This expanse of open countryside included a valley drained by a little stream, groves, grottoes, and a temple dedicated to Ceres.[8] Today it is still possible to visit the second-century temple, which looks out on what is very likely a survival of a sacred ilex grove, visible at the right in the photograph. Set into the hillside on which the temple sits is a grotto, the so-called Nymphaeum of Egeria, which was clearly part of the overall landscape composition (Fig. 7). Of particular interest is the reclining statue of the fluvial divinity from beneath which the water originally issued in three streams, recalling Ovid's description of Tempe. In each of the examples considered thus far, religious associations—personifications, even—are considered necessary complements to the natural forms themselves.

With the fall of the Roman Empire sacred associations in landscape came to be construed as demonic manifestations of evil by Christian reformers, who, like Saint Benedict, actively campaigned in the country-

6. F. W. Deichmann, "Die Entstehungszeit von Salvatorkirche und Clitumnus Tempel bei Spoleto," *Mitteilungen des deutschen archaeologischen Instituts* (Römische Abteilung), LVIII, 1943, 106–148.

7. Pliny the Younger, *Letters*, VIII, 8 (W. Melmoth, trans., London and New York, 1915, II, 115–117).

8. G. Lugli, "Studi topografici intorno alle antiche ville suburbane," *Bullettino della commissione archeologica communale di Roma*, III, 1925, 120–134.

side, cutting down sacred groves and destroying temples to build monasteries in their place, as at Montecassino. It is only with the Renaissance that we see a revival of interest in the landscape of allusion, based, of course, on the careful and loving study of classical literature and the substantive remains of ancient villas. Perhaps the finest single example of this revival is the Villa Madama in Rome, designed by Raphael for Pope Clement VII in 1516. Thanks to the recent discovery of Raphael's written program for the Villa, we know that his design was intended to breathe three-dimensional life into classical texts—Pliny's descriptions of his Laurentine and Tuscan villas—and in the process to re-establish a direct and meaningful relationship between villa architecture and the surrounding landscape.[9] A revealing illustration of Raphael's fidelity to his literary sources is the circular courtyard at the center of the villa, visible in Antonio da Sangallo the Younger's plan (Fig. 8). This is the result of Raphael's working with an imperfect edition of Pliny's letters in which the portico of his Laurentine villa was described as having the shape of the letter O. More accurate editions, which only became available in the nineteenth century, make it clear that Pliny's portico was actually shaped like the letter D, and thus was a semicircular—not a circular—exedra.[10] If Raphael's error reveals how closely he followed his literary sources, his design, on the other hand, was anything but a slavish copy of Roman precedent. Indeed, the Villa Madama constitutes one of the first modern instances of a circular courtyard applied to a secular building, a brilliant exercise in classical design suggested by the architectural forms of Antiquity but transcending mere imitation: in effect an inspired "translation" expressing the spirit, if not the letter of Pliny's description.

The English Augustans viewed the architectural forms of Classical Antiquity primarily through the medium of Renaissance "translations" similar to Raphael's which had been codified in the treatises of Serlio, Palladio, Vignola, and others. Likewise, their vision of the landscape was based on classical texts, many of which had been visually translated —not illustrated—by seventeenth-century painters like Claude and Poussin. Such a visual translation is Claude's *Aeneas on Delos* of 1673 (Fig. 9). The eighteenth-century landscape of allusion, therefore, had as its two primary sources poetry and painting. Landscape gardening, of course, is an artistic medium in its own right, in which the forms of Nature are molded by man and given meaning through association with works of architecture and sculpture. While it is obvious that Pope's reference to "laughing Ceres" or Cobham's placement of a temple of

9. P. Foster, "Raphael on the Villa Madama: The Text of a Lost Letter," *Römisches Jahrbuch für Kunstgeschichte*, XI, 1967/68, 307–312.

10. H. Tanzer, *The Villas of Pliny the Younger* (New York, 1924).

Bacchus at Stowe were not motivated by religious piety, such sacred allusions played an essential role in determining the iconography of eighteenth-century landscape gardens. Furthermore, in many instances such sacred allusions were topographical in nature as well, and thus provided an added level of classical association. That this occurred at all is because the most influential garden theorists, men like Pope and Addison, were poets steeped in classical literature. Gardens laid out following their principles tended to express an ideal poetic conception of Nature which constituted the primary stimulus for what became, in the process, a revolutionary visual aesthetic.

While the most influential English landscape theorists and gardeners were at their ease with a volume of Latin verse and often were architectural dilettantes of considerable erudition as well, this did not mean that they were content merely to illustrate specific classical texts or erect precise reproductions of Roman buildings. Literal copies of classical temples only began to appear in English gardens after the middle of the eighteenth century.[11] For the generation of Pope and Kent it was enough to suggest a correspondence without realizing absolute visual congruity; indeed, to do so would have been the death of poetry and the poetic landscape of the eighteenth century. It is important to view the concern of the English Augustans for generalized evocative topographical allusions against the background of their Roman predecessors. If the appearance and nomenclature of English gardens recalled Clitumnus or Praeneste, and by extension the order and grandeur of Augustan Rome, the gardens of Pliny's day reflected a similar regard for yet more venerable sites, like Tempe, with its associations of a golden age of pastoral ease.

As early as Varro we find testimony to the fashion among wealthy Romans for attaching exotic names to their villas: ". . . they do not think they have a real villa unless it rings with many resounding Greek names. . . ."[12] The Latin word for gardener, *topiarius*, is, after all, derived from the Greek word meaning place. We know that Cicero's friend Atticus, at his villa in Epirus, had an *Amaltheum*, named after the legendary site on Mount Ida where Zeus was brought up by his stepmother Amalthea. Atticus' Amaltheum comprised a grove, a stream, and a sanctuary, and together these clearly formed a planned landscape composition which Cicero was anxious to imitate on the grounds of his own villa.[13] In

11. The Doric Temple at Hagley Park, based on Stuart and Revett's published drawings of the Theseum in the Athenian Agora, is the product of a later, more self-consciously Neoclassical sensibility.

12. M. T. Varro, *On Agriculture*, II, 2 (W. D. Hooper, trans., Cambridge, Mass., 1934, p. 309).

13. Cicero, *Letters to Atticus*, I, 16; II, 1. (Winstedt, trans., New York, 1912, I, 65; 111).

another of Cicero's letters we read that Brutus' villa at Lanuvium included an *Eurotas* and a Persian porch.[14] Brutus' *Eurotas* was a reference to a river which flowed through Sparta; his Persian porch to a portico commemorating the Spartan victory over the Persians. Brutus' choice of Spartan landmarks for inclusion in his garden no doubt reflects more than his familiarity with the site. It can be interpreted as a personal statement expressing political and philosophical affinities with Spartan liberty, as contrasted to the servility of the Persians under their absolute monarchy. George Clarke has shown how similar moral and political values were expressed in eighteenth-century English gardens, most notably at Stowe.[15]

While nothing survives of Atticus' *Amaltheum* and Brutus' portico, a later Imperial example of the same kind of topographical associations used to enrich the landscape does survive, at least in part. We learn from a Late Antique collection of Imperial biographies that Hadrian's Villa near Tivoli included a number of structures intended to recall famous places the emperor had visited in the course of his wide-ranging tours of inspection throughout the Roman Empire:

> His villa at Tibur was marvellously constructed, and he actually gave to parts of it the names of provinces and places of greatest renown, calling them, for instance, Lyceum, Academia, Prytaneum, Canopus, Poecile and Tempe.[16]

It is possible, today, to identify certain of the landscape-related complexes with a degree of certainty. To the east of the Villa the land drops off sharply to form a valley of great natural beauty, and at a number of places temples and towers were erected to provide lofty viewpoints out over the surrounding countryside. The circular colonnade of one of these structures, identified as the Temple of Venus (Fig. 10), appears at the right of the reconstruction model in Figure 11. It seems reasonable to identify the valley which it surveys as yet another Roman evocation of the Grecian Vale of Tempe, so beloved of the pastoral poets.

If we are on somewhat less secure ground in identifying other surviving portions of Hadrian's Villa with the famous places mentioned by the emperor's biographer, it is due at least in part to one extremely important characteristic of these classical allusions. There is no evidence to support the view that any of these structures were literal imitations of the older monuments whose names they carried. To the contrary, all were new and innovative designs, often bearing only the most general visual relationship to their namesakes. This can be seen in another

14. *Ibid.*, xv, 9 (Vol. iii, 319).

15. G. Clarke, "Grecian Taste and Gothic Virtue: Lord Cobham's Gardening Programme and its Iconography," *Apollo*, xcvii, 1973, 566–571.

16. *Scriptores Historiae Augustae*, Hadrian, xvi, 5.

example from the Villa, the *Canopus*, named after the shrine of Serapis near Alexandria (Fig. 12). The row of shops, set into the hillside at the right, sheet of water, and dark terminal concavity are enough to suggest an analogy to the exotic eastern sanctuary, which was approached by a canal. Hadrian's free and imaginative architectural translations, and his passion for collecting, as it were, reproductions of buildings and places whose very names ring with hallowed associations, clearly anticipate the attitude of numerous well-travelled English lords, whose gardens were sown with allusions to particularly memorable stopping points on their Grand Tours.

The English taste for topographical allusions in their gardens began well before the eighteenth century, as can be seen at Albury Park, in Surrey (Fig. 13). John Evelyn's diary records that he accompanied Henry Howard, Duke of Norfolk ". . . to his villa at Alburie where I designed for him the plot for his Canale and Garden, with a Crypta through the hill . . . such a Pausilippe is no where in England besides."[17] By crypta Evelyn clearly means a vaulted Roman portico, or *cryptoporticus*, like the long gallery at Posillipo near Naples, which was destroyed in the nineteenth century. Evelyn's cryptoporticus, however, still survives at Albury Park, as do the monumental terracing and traces of the original plantings of acanthus, box, and bay—eloquent testimony to the early enthusiasm for classical landscape forms. In the next century, at Rousham Park near Oxford, William Kent constructed a massive arched portico which was called Praeneste (Fig. 14), because it suggested the ponderous vaulted substructures of the Roman shrine of Fortuna Primigenia at Praeneste (Fig. 15). To Horace Walpole, the adjacent Vale of Venus at Rousham (Fig. 16) called to mind another classical allusion:

> The whole is as elegant and antique as if the emperor Julian had selected the most pleasing solitude about Daphne to enjoy a philosophical retirement.[18]

The significance of allusions—literary, sacred, topographical, and historical—in the landscape gardens of the English Augustans can be further traced at Stourhead, in Wiltshire. Kenneth Woodbridge has remarked on the obvious similarity of these gardens to Clitumnus.[19] It is likely that Henry Hoare visited the classical site shortly before work was begun on his garden at Stourhead, which, like its classical counterpart, follows the curving perimeter of a lake and contains numerous temples

17. W. Bray, ed., *The Diary of John Evelyn* (London, 1818), pp. 412, 443.

18. H. Walpole, *The History of Modern Taste in Gardening* (1780). Passage quoted by J. D. Hunt and P. Willis, *The Genius of the Place* (London, 1975), p. 315.

19. K. Woodbridge, *Landscape and Antiquity. Aspects of English Culture at Stourhead, 1718–1838* (Oxford, 1970).

and shrines, including one based on the Pantheon (Fig. 17).[20] At one point along the itinerary is a grotto recalling that of the Nymph Egeria, within which are placed statues of a river god and a sleeping nymph (Figs. 18 and 19). The former is a sculptural adaptation of Salvator Rosa's personification of the Tiber in his painting representing *The Dream of Aeneas* (ca. 1662), while the latter is based on a well-known Hellenistic statue of Ariadne. Beneath the fountain of the sleeping nymph, which in turn reflects a Renaissance prototype,[21] is inscribed Pope's translation of the classical epigram (since proven a forgery) with which he hoped to grace his own grotto at Twickenham:

> Nymph of the Grot these sacred springs I keep
> And to the murmur of these waters sleep;
> Ah! spare my slumbers, gently tread the cave,
> And drink in silence or in silence lave.[22]

The Stourhead nymph, the visual counterpart of the nymph in Pope's verse, literally ". . . tells the waters or to rise or fall."[23] It is indeed hard to imagine a clearer example of the vital relationship between literary and visual allusions in eighteenth-century English landscape gardens; Greek sculpture and Roman architecture, Renaissance fountains and Baroque painting, contemporary verse and (presumed) classical poetry, all combine to produce an experience which appeals to the senses and the intellect alike.

Stourhead provides an excellent example of how other monuments with distinctly non-classical associations were woven into the landscape texture to form a rich allusive fabric. The Bristol Cross (Fig. 20), a fourteenth-century market crucifix, contributes a Christian element to this sacred landscape as it looks out at the temples of Hercules, Apollo, and Flora which grace the lake shore. Furthermore, it calls to mind both local and national associations, as does another monument placed at some distance from the lake: Alfred's Tower (Fig. 21). This brick structure was erected on the very hillside where by tradition King Alfred deployed his forces in 878 to repel the Danish invaders. In function it is a belvedere, a vantage point offering pleasing prospects out over the Salisbury Plain. It also represents an important English contribution to

20. Work on Stourhead began shortly after 1741 and continued for the next half century. The monuments discussed here constitute successive additions to the original scheme: the Pantheon (ca. 1754), the Bristol Cross (re-erected 1768), Alfred's Tower (1772), the Grotto (1779).

21. E. B. MacDougall, "The Sleeping Nymph: Origins of a Humanist Fountain Type," *The Art Bulletin*, LVII, 1975, 357–365.

22. A. Pope, Letter to E. Blount in date of 6/2/1725 (*The Works of Alexander Pope*, London, 1766, VIII, 38).

23. Pope, "Epistle to Lord Burlington."

the landscape of allusion, the inclusion of secular monuments to important national and historical figures.

An early and monumental example of a great landscape garden built around specific historical allusions is Blenheim. The British nation's gift to the Duke of Marlborough in gratitude for his Continental victories was already hallowed ground, for it incorporated the ancient manor of Woodstock, where English kings had hunted since Saxon times. Vanbrugh's Baroque palace grandly looks out towards the Victory Column surmounted by Marlborough's statue (Fig. 22). The inscription on the column's base recounts the commander's martial feats in the service of his country. Even Nature herself was made to express this theme: the formal gardens were originally laid out on a bastioned parterre and the trees framing the vista to the column recall the battle lines formed by the opposing armies at the Battle of Blenheim. At Blenheim and in other English gardens we begin to see celebrated not just the divine manifestations of Nature, but also such historical figures and events as parallel the example and achievements of the Roman Augustans.

Of all the eighteenth-century English landscape gardens, Stowe is certainly the most complex, offering the greatest possible variety of vistas expressing a multitude of themes, poetic, political, and moral—truly "A work to wonder at." The pride of Stowe is its rich display of temples and related garden structures, which once numbered close to forty (Fig. 23). Horace Walpole, after enumerating Stowe's principal monuments, commented that

> . . . all these images crowd upon one's memory, and add visionary personages to the charming scenes, that are so enriched with fanes and temples, that the real prospects are little less than visions themselves.[24]

While many of Stowe's temples carried the names of classical divinities, others were dedicated to such ideal abstractions as Liberty, Friendship, and Virtue, and still others suggested associations which not only commemorated historical personages and events, but commented on contemporary politics as well. At the hands of the English Augustans the landscape of allusion became a fully developed artistic medium in its own right, no longer a mere adjunct of poetry, providing three-dimensional illustrations of appropriate texts, but capable of expressing a wide range of themes and values.

One such theme, treating the Elysian Fields, found expression in eighteenth-century elegiac poetry and landscape gardens. Here again, it is possible to trace a number of extremely revealing parallel expressions of this theme in the literature and art of Classical Antiquity which shed

24. H. Walpole, Letter to G. Montague in date of 7/7/1770 (quoted by C. Hussey, *English Gardens and Landscapes 1700–1750*, London, 1967, p. 113).

new light on its use and interpretation by the English Augustans. The Underworld is an important *topos* in Classical literature, the most famous descriptions being those of Homer and Virgil. Among the series of first-century frescoes known as the Odyssey Landscapes is one scene depicting Odysseus' descent into Hades to consult the seer Tiresias (Fig. 24).[25] In the middleground we see the shades of fallen heroes gathering round the sacrificial trench which has been dug by Odysseus. To the left is a reclining personification of the river Styx and dominating the whole scene is a natural arch through which a ghostly light slants. The artist has done more than merely illustrate Homer's verses; he has realized an atmosphere which is at once the product of the unusual landscape setting and the expressive illumination. Like the personification of Mount Ida in the other Roman landscape fresco we have considered, the presence of the river god in this scene provides at once a specific identity and a sacred context for the event depicted.

The travails of Odysseus were also the theme of a great marine garden attached to a villa in all probability built for the Emperor Tiberius at Sperlonga, halfway along the coast between Rome and Naples.[26] Our understanding of the iconography of this garden, which centers on a large natural grotto (Fig. 25), is by no means complete. What is certain, however, is that sculpture was used to recreate a number of scenes from the Odyssey, one of which was Odysseus' shipwreck. It seems clear that the principal group, composed of Odysseus and his shipmates clinging to the stern of their sinking ship, was set up at water level at the middle of the grotto. By mechanical means the water could be drained from the basin, causing a violent vortex to froth about the statues, which, in the eery light, created a dramatic climax to a pleasant walk through the garden.[27] There is no evidence that there was another group representing the descent to Hades, though such a scene is readily conjectured. Nonetheless, the Sperlonga grotto does provide precious documentation of the existence of an elaborate garden iconography based on a literary theme in the first century. Moreover, such themes were particularly appropriate to the kind of garden which unfolds slowly, one piece at a time; for as the visitor's programmed itinerary progresses, so the literary events are made to unfold, often involving unexpected sequences.

The visit to the Underworld as one part of a garden itinerary appears to have occurred in at least one more Roman garden for which evidence

25. P. H. von Blanckenhagen, "The Odyssey Frieze," *Mitteilungen des deutschen archaeologischen Instituts* (Römische Abteilung), LXX, 1963, 100–146.

26. G. Jacobi, *L'Antro di Tiberio a Sperlonga* (Rome, 1963).

27. J. Felbermeyer, "Sperlonga, The Ship of Odysseus," *Archaeology*, XXIV, 1971, 136–145.

survives. This is Hadrian's Villa, which we have already encountered. After enumerating the famous monuments of the ancient world to which Hadrian alluded in his villa, the emperor's biographer went on to say that in order not to omit anything, Hadrian "even made Hades."[28] At its southern end the Vale of Tempe narrows considerably and beyond one finds the entrance to what in all likelihood was Hadrian's recreation of the Underworld (Fig. 26). The contrast between the rich open countryside without and the cool, shady realm within could not be more pronounced—the one teeming with verdant life, the other still and void of any living thing. The galleries making up this Underworld itinerary measure some 2,800 feet in length and at one point were interrupted by the waters of an underground spring, a natural feature which may well have been exploited to represent the Styx. While the English Augustans never produced a garden Hades of such grandiose proportions, their interest in the theme, and in particular with the contrast between fertility and mortality in nature, was clearly anticipated in these Roman examples.

The Underworld played an important part in at least one garden of the Italian Renaissance: Bomarzo, which was laid out by Vicino Orsini around the middle of the sixteenth century.[29] The garden at Bomarzo comprises a number of landscape incidents which were intended to be experienced sequentially, several of which were apparently linked to evoke a descent into Hades. Dominating the uppermost terrace of the gardens is a mysterious structure, half mausoleum, half funerary chapel, ringed by a circle of stone markers adorned by death heads. From this upper level of the tomb one descends to the mouth of Hades itself, passing along the way a statue of its guardian, Cerberus (Figs. 27 and 28). Playing on Dante, and in keeping with the bizarre sense of humor of the patron, the inscription above the gaping mouth of Hell reads "Forsake all cares you who enter." In close proximity to the entrance to Hades are statues of fantastic animals and colossal men locked in combat. These struggling figures may well be references to the funeral contests which play an important part in the epic verse of Homer and Virgil. In their willful distortions of classical precedent and proportion they call to mind the satirical games which figure so prominently in the Underworld sequence of Pope's mock epic, "The Dunciad." Orsini referred to his garden as a "bosco sacro," or sacred grove, and while many of the allusions it contains are distinctly anti-classical, nonetheless, his ability to shock and amuse his audience was based on a defiance

28. *Scriptores Historiae Augustae*, Hadrian, XVI, 5.

29. L. Benevolo, "Saggio d'interpretazione storica del Sacro Bosco," *Quaderni dell' Istituto di Storia dell' Architettura*, nos. 7–9, 1955, 61–73. There is no evidence that Bomarzo was known to eighteenth-century landscape gardeners.

of the expectations they had formed through their familiarity with classical texts and more orthodox Renaissance gardens.

Another elegiac theme of interest to the English Augustans was introduced by Virgil in the *Eclogues* and taken up again in the seventeenth century by Poussin, who gave it compelling pictorial form. This is the subject known as "Et in Arcadia Ego" after Panofsky's masterful study of its origins and visual evolution.[30] The theme of the Golden Age was an important expression of the Augustan myth but here it is rendered more poignant by the introduction of an allusion to man's mortality. "Even in Arcady," that mythical realm of happiness and perfection, "I, Death, hold sway"; this is Virgil's message, and Poussin's too. In Poussin's second painting of this subject, four Arcadian shepherds have happened on a sepulchral monument, and are absorbed in the contemplation of the idea of mortality (Fig. 29). They are not terrified or dismayed by this unexpected discovery; rather they discuss it calmly among themselves, the tomb and their melancholy attitudes setting the mood in this exquisite landscape composition. This is the very mood of Virgil's Fifth Eclogue, so effectively expressed in Dryden's translation:

> A lasting monument to Daphnis raise
> With this inscription to record his praise:
> "Daphnis, the fields delight, the shepherd's love,
> Renown'd on earth and deifi'd above;
> Whose flocks excelled the fairest on the plains,
> But less than he himself surpassed the swains."[31]

This is also the elegiac mood of eighteenth-century English Elysiums which occupy an important place in a number of landscape gardens, particularly at Stowe.

In 1733, at the very center of Lord Cobham's estate of Stowe, William Kent began to lay out the Elysian Fields. One of Kent's first steps was to dam up a natural rivulet which drained this declivity to create the sluggish, reed-clogged stream identified as the Styx, which is visible in Figures 30 and 31. On one side of the Styx, set high above the stream, is the Temple of Ancient Virtue, a spare Ionic structure expressing in architecture the austerity of the Greek heroes whose busts were enshrined within (Fig. 30). Three of these—Homer, Socrates, and Epaminondas—had also appeared in Pope's "Temple of Fame," while the fourth, the Spartan lawgiver Lycurgus, was included for his associations with liberty. Just as Brutus had invoked the Spartans in his garden, so the

30. E. Panofsky, "Et in Arcadia Ego: Poussin and the Elegiac Tradition," *Meaning in the Visual Arts* (Harmondsworth, 1970), pp. 340–367.

31. Virgil, *Eclogues*, v, 42ff.

English Augustans identified themselves with Sparta, casting the French in the role of the Persians.[32] There is a general similarity between the siting of the Temple of Ancient Virtue and that of the so-called Temple of Sibyl at Tivoli, which was well known to Kent. This similarity would have been even more apparent in the eighteenth century, when smaller shade trees served to emphasize the relative height of the temple.

If so far the mood of Kent's Elysian Fields has been profoundly classical, Virgilian with only a trace of an English accent, its second component breaks with the steady elegiac measure and brings the whole landscape composition more into line with a satire by Pope. This is the Temple of Modern Virtue, built as a ruin, in shambles and presided over by the headless statue of Walpole, the archenemy of Cobham's Whig opposition (Fig. 31). Unfortunately, this crucial monument of the Elysian Fields no longer survives, but we are familiar with it from numerous descriptions and prints. Surely this is the contemporary counterpart in gardening of Pope's mock heroic visit to the Underworld in "The Dunciad." That this is so is not in the least surprising, of course, since Pope was consulted on the work at Stowe.

On the opposite side of the Styx Kent placed the third, and culminating monument of the Elysian Fields, the Temple of British Worthies (Fig. 32). This is laid out in the form of an exedra articulated by sixteen niches containing the busts of famous English kings, philosophers, writers, and architects. The empty oval niche in the pyramid once contained a head of Mercury, the messenger god who leads the souls of heroes to the Elysian Fields. As George Clarke has shown, the selection of the Worthies was determined by the political views of Cobham, and together they represented an ideal standard against which to measure contemporary leaders. In the Temple of British Worthies the visitor is confronted with an eighteenth-century visual counterpart to the Underworld scene in the *Aeneid*, where Rome's glorious future is foretold by the shades of her heroic past.

The Elysian Fields at Stowe remain the most complete expression in gardening of the elegiac themes we have traced back to Classical Antiquity. By no means, however, should Stowe be considered as unique in this respect, for there are a number of other eighteenth-century landscape gardens in which the contrast of fertility and mortality in nature plays a major role, and in which certain elements of an Underworld itinerary are present. One of these gardens—Rousham Park, where we have already seen the arcade recalling Praeneste—was taking form at the hands of Kent at approximately the same time as was Stowe.

32. Cf. George Clarke's discussion of Richard Glover's poem "Leonidas" (1737) in "Moral Gardening," no. 10 in the series of articles on the history of Stowe beginning March, 1967, in *The Stoic*, p. 118.

Large cinerary urns line the terrace in front of Praeneste, a pyramid graces one of the lower walks, and a description of 1750 mentions "Proserpine's Cave," which boasted statues of Pluto, Proserpine, and other attendant figures.[33] Indeed, sculpture plays an important part in Kent's design for Rousham, where statues have been placed with telling effect throughout the garden (Fig. 33). The view from the terrace supported by Praeneste has as a dominating foreground feature Sheemaker's copy of the *Dying Gaul* (Fig. 34). Set against the wide expanse of peaceful landscape, this statue introduces an element of contrast, a melancholy meditation on mortality.[34] Much as in a painting by Poussin, the figures and landscape work together to evoke an atmosphere at once timeless and transitory.

Kent was not the only landscape designer to introduce elegiac themes into the iconography of eighteenth-century English gardens. Part of the circuit of the garden at Stourhead included a miniature Hades, the Virgilian inspiration for which is confirmed by a letter in which Henry Hoare quotes from the *Aeneid*: "I have made the passage up from the Sousterrain Serpentine & will make it easier of access *facile descensus Averno*."[35] However, it is at Castle Howard in Yorkshire that we see the most monumental expression of Elysium. Here, from 1726 onward, Charles Howard, Third Earl of Carlisle, opened up a vast landscape composition to the east of his newly completed house, which was conceived on a truly epic scale. Along the brow of a hill overlooking the valley below, Carlisle had Sir John Vanbrugh build a viewing platform which he crowned with the elegant Temple of the Four Winds (Fig. 35). From this vantage point the observer can survey an ample arc of landscape anchored at one end by the Earl's own Mausoleum (Fig. 36). At the center of this vast panorama (but not visible in Figure 36) is a pyramidal monument to the third Earl's ancestor Lord William Howard, which is silhouetted on the skyline nearly one mile distant. Anchoring the opposite end of the vista is the cupola of Castle Howard itself. The Mausoleum, intended to contain the remains of Carlisle and his descendants, was designed by Nicholas Hawkesmoore (Fig. 37).[36] In placing his own memorial in a landscape setting studded with other family and funereal associations Lord Carlisle went further than any

33. K. Woodbridge, "William Kent's Gardening: The Rousham Letters," *Apollo*, C, 1974, 289.

34. The proprietor of Rousham, General James Dormer, was mortally ill when the statue was set up in 1741. There is a preparatory study by Kent depicting Sheemaker's statue placed on a sarcophagus.

35. Letter of Henry Hoare to Lord Bruce, 12/23/1765. Quoted by Woodbridge, *Landscape and Antiquity*, p. 35.

36. Hawkesmoore's design is an imaginative adaptation of an ancient Roman monument, the Trophy of Augustus at La Turbie.

other of his contemporaries in realizing an Elysium which was at once a sublime poetic and pictorial composition and a living reality.

The rich resonance of English Augustan poetry and landscape design is clearly as much the product of such expressions of individual concerns and tastes as it is a conscious harkening back to the classical past. Were the Elysium at Castle Howard or the temples at Stowe merely identical copies of specific classical prototypes they could never convey the multiple levels of meaning which make them so satisfying. The process of adapting, not simply adopting, the forms of the past to suit their own times and whimsy granted the English Augustans the opportunity to provide new interpretations and reverberations of what had come before. The dynamic translation of classical ideals, and particularly poetic themes of literature and landscape, into English eighteenth-century terms inevitably yielded images which were evocative and revealing of both Augustan ages.

Fig. 1. Rome, Ara Pacis, Terra Mater relief (Fototeca Unione)

Fig. 2. Primaporta Augustus, Vatican Museum (Alinari/Editorial Photocolor Archives)

FIG. 3. Paris on Mount Ida, fresco from Pompeii now in the Museo Nazionale, Naples (Smith College Slide and Photograph Collection)

FIG. 4. Tivoli, Temple of Sibyl (Photo J.P.)

FIG. 5. The Temple of Clitumnus (Alinari/Editorial Photocolor Archives)

FIG. 6. Rome, The Triopion or Estate of Herodius Atticus, temple and ilex grove (Photo J.P.)

FIG. 7. Rome, Nymphaeum of Egeria (Alinari/Editorial Photocolor Archives)

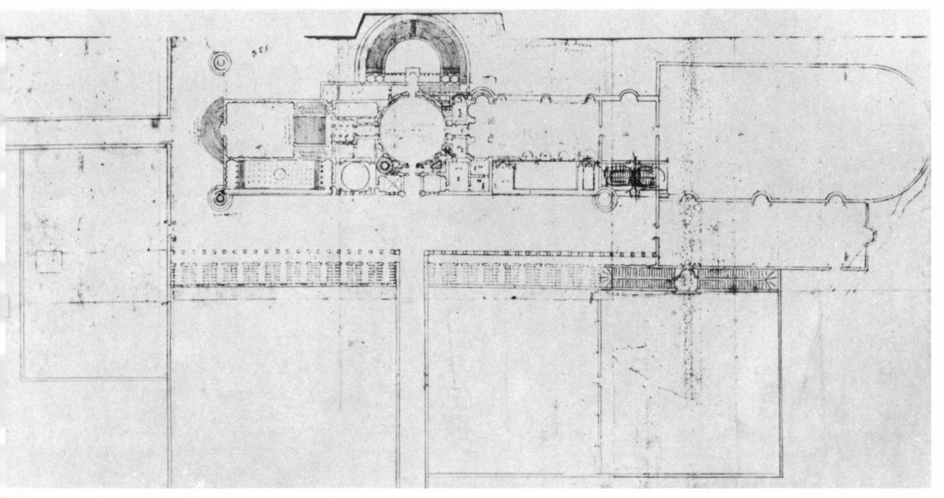

FIG. 8. Rome, Villa Madama, plan by Antonio da Sangallo the Younger, Uffizi 314a (Smith College Slide and Photograph Collection)

FIG. 9. Claude Lorraine, *Aeneas on Delos* (1673), London, National Gallery (Smith College Slide and Photograph Collection)

FIG. 10. Tivoli, Hadrian's Villa, Temple of Venus (Fototeca Unione)

FIG. 11. Tivoli, Hadrian's Villa, model (Photo J.P.)

FIG. 12. Tivoli, Hadrian's Villa, Canopus (Photo J.P.)

FIG. 13. Surrey, Albury Park, terraces designed by John Evelyn (Country Life)

FIG. 14. Oxfordshire, Rousham Park, Praeneste (Photo J.P.)

FIG. 15. Palestrina (ancient Praeneste), Shrine of Fortuna Primigenia (Fototeca Unione)

FIG. 16. Oxfordshire, Rousham Park, Vale of Venus (Country Life)

FIG. 17. Wiltshire, Stourhead, The Pantheon (Photo J.P.)

FIG. 18. Wiltshire, Stourhead, Grot
River God (Photo J.P.)

FIG. 19. Wiltshire, Stourhead, Grotto, Sleeping Nymph (Country Life)

FIG. 20. Wiltshire, Stourhead, Bristol Cross (Country Life)

FIG. 21. Wiltshire, Stourhead, Alfred's Tower (Country Life)

FIG. 22. Oxfordshire, Blenheim, Victory Column (Oxfordshire County Libraries)

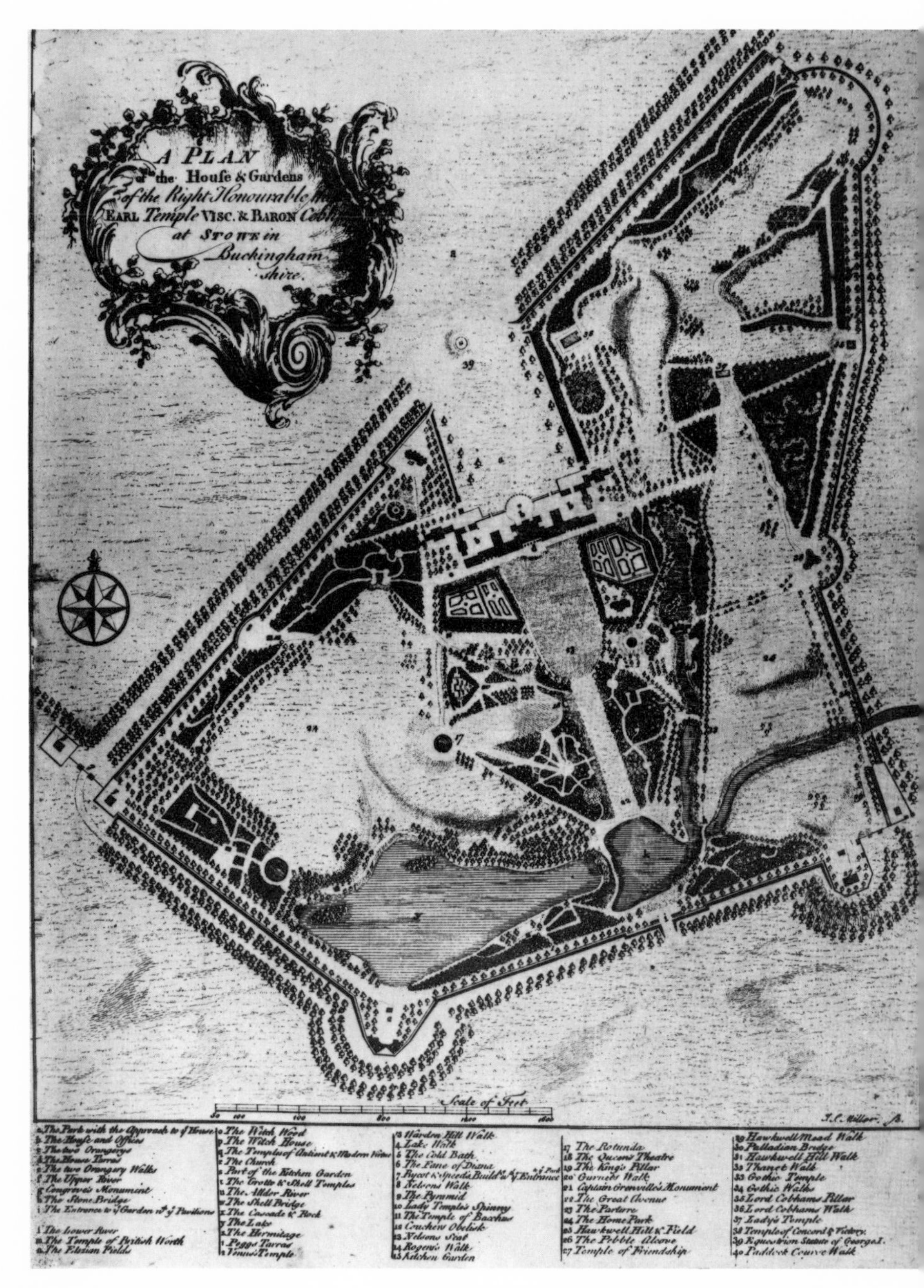

FIG. 23. Buckinghamshire, Stowe, plan, 1769 (National Monuments Record, London)

Fig. 24. Odysseus' Descent to Hades, Roman landscape fresco, Vatican Museums (Smith College Slide and Photograph Collection)

Fig. 25. Sperlonga, Grotto of Tiberius (Fototeca Unione)

Fig. 26. Tivoli, Hadrian's Villa, Inferi (Photo J.P.)

FIG. 27. Bomarzo, Bosco Sacro, Cerberus (Gabinetto fotografico nazionale)

IG. 28. Bomarzo, Bosco Sacro, Mouth of Hell (Gabinetto fotografico nazionale)

IG. 29. Nicolas Poussin,
in Arcadia Ego (ca.
50), Paris, Louvre
mith College Slide and
otograph Collection)

FIG. 30. Buckinghamshire, Stowe, Elysian Fields, Temple of Ancient Virtue (Photo J.P.)

FIG. 31. Buckinghamshire, Stowe, Elysian Fields, Temple of Modern Virtue (Photo by permission of the British Library)

FIG. 32. Buckinghamshire, Stowe, Elysian Fields, Temple of British Worthies (Photo J.P.)

FIG. 33. Oxfordshire, Rousham Park, Vale of Venus, Van Nost's statue of Pan overlooking the Upper Cascade (Photo J.P.)

FIG. 34. Oxfordshire, Rousham Park, Sheemaker's Dying Gaul (Country Life)

FIG. 35. Yorkshire, Castle Howard, Temple of the Four Winds (Photo J.P.)

FIG. 36. Yorkshire, Castle Howard, View from the Temple of the Four Winds (Photo J.P.)

FIG. 37. Yorkshire, Castle Howard, Hawkesmoore's Mausoleum (Photo J.P.)

THE FOUNDING FATHERS AND ANTIQUITY: A SELECTIVE PASSION

The Founding Fathers and Antiquity: A Selective Passion

LOUIS COHN-HAFT

WILLIAM BYRD OF WESTOVER (in Virginia) died at the age of seventy in 1744, so he is too early to be called a "Founding Father." But here, anyway, is a translation of the beginning of his letter proposing marriage to Maria Taylor, who became his second wife. The original is in Greek: "When I thought you knew only your mother-tongue, I was passionately in love with you; but when I learned that you also spoke Greek, the tongue of the Muses, I went completely crazy about you."[1]

Love of the classics seems to affect people that way and I should not be surprised if many of us connected with the enterprise of this Alumnae College are capable of similar flights. I know that I myself am deeply moved to be included in this occasion which does honor to the classical world and to Phyllis Lehmann, of whom I have had the privilege of being a colleague at Smith for twenty-five years. It is a family affair in another way, too, for among the Founding Fathers, the most scholarly and profound classicist was Thomas Jefferson; and on this side of Jefferson's many-sided genius Mrs. Lehmann's late husband, the very distinguished classical scholar, Karl Lehmann, some thirty-one years ago published a pioneering book that is still one of the essential works for *my* topic.[2]

I shall not return to William Byrd, for he is too early for me. My topic is the Founding Fathers, and my time span is primarily the last quarter of the eighteenth century. A certain flexibility is needed, for many of the Founding Fathers were quite young when the Declaration of Inde-

The author gratefully acknowledges the help of the following colleagues: Stanley Elkins, Lawrence Fink, Donald Robinson, Stanley Rothman, Allen Weinstein, and R. Jackson Wilson.

1. Cited in Richard M. Gummere, *The American Colonial Mind and the Classical Tradition* (Cambridge, Mass.: Harvard University Press, 1963), pp. 85–86.

2. Karl Lehmann, *Thomas Jefferson, American Humanist* (New York: Macmillan Co., 1947).

pendence was promulgated and some of them lived a long time thereafter. It is one of history's attractive coincidences that John Adams and Thomas Jefferson both died on July 4, 1826, on the *fiftieth* anniversary of the Declaration.

Modern scholarship has now established the classical attachments of the Founding Fathers. But although it was not possible for these eighteenth-century public men to be entirely indifferent to or ignorant of classical antiquity, the degree of their love, their knowledge, and their use of the classics varied greatly.

At one extreme is a Jefferson. In old age, in the famous correspondence with Adams, Jefferson expresses his gratitude to his father for his classical training. "I would not exchange this attainment," he then says, "for anything which I could then have acquired and have since acquired." "Classics," Adams agreed, were "indispensable."[3]

On the other side, Benjamin Franklin, while not hostile to classical learning, emphasized as early as 1749 the value of other areas of knowledge; and at the extreme opposite pole from Jefferson was Benjamin Rush, who conducted what might be called a regular campaign of hostility to the classics. In 1791 Rush wrote to the principal of the Academy of Alexandria, Virginia, to express his delight that of the school's ninety boys only nineteen were studying Latin.[4]

Devotion to the world of Classical Antiquity lasted longer in America than in Europe, and as I have observed, modern scholarship has established not only the ubiquity but also the intensity of classical knowledge in the minds of the Founding Fathers.

Let me say a few things about that scholarship. The study of the classicism of the Founding Fathers cuts across two very separate fields. The American specialist of the Revolutionary Period is likely to be quite gingerly in his evaluation of classical learning, being, in all probability, without Latin (to say nothing of Greek) himself, and finding it hard to believe that busy public men in a time of turmoil could turn from the wheeling and dealing of politics to the comfortable enjoyment of Greek and Latin literature, often in the original. The classicist, on the other hand, has forgotten whatever United States history he learned in high school, and feeling himself an embattled survivor of a finer era, will tend to exaggerate the influence of the classics. In his delight at discovering that Jefferson's command of Greek and Latin was as good as, probably better than, his own, he will often forget that Jefferson (and his contemporaries) also knew modern literature, modern political theory, modern books on the sciences and agriculture—to say nothing of the

3. This exchange is cited in Gummere, *Colonial Mind*, p. 193.

4. Cited in Meyer Reinhold, *The Classick Pages* (University Park: Pennsylvania State University, 1975), p. 14.

Bible—and that these varied sources of knowledge were put to varied use.

Because of the need for the two types of specialist, progress has been slow and cautious, but over the years since the first serious inquiries appeared at the end of the 1930's, substantial headway has been made. In the 50's and early 60's, Richard M. Gummere carried the study to a new level with a series of articles and books focussing his classicist's skills upon a tremendously larger acquaintance with the eighteenth-century sources than had previously been brought to bear. Others have made important contributions. Most recently American classicists launched a program of research in connection with the celebration of the Bicentennial. The most significant work to come out of this effort so far is a volume published in 1975, *The Classick Pages*, by Meyer Reinhold. The book consists of selections from those Greek and Latin classics most often cited by the Founding Fathers, in the translations that were most used at the time, and also excerpts from the most popular eighteenth-century books on the history of the Greeks and Romans. The texts are accompanied by notes and preceded by an introduction which together provide a remarkably thorough review of all aspects of the subject and a dependable survey of the scholarship up to 1975.

I think I do not do too great an injustice in summarizing the results of the scholarly enterprise thus far as a general downgrading of the influence and importance of the ancient world by the United States historians in contrast to the emphasis of the classicists upon the decisive value of the classics for the ideas of the Founding Fathers.

Let me not hesitate to say where I stand in this matter. Although a classicist, I believe that in general the American historians are more nearly accurate in their perception. A phrase of Bernard Bailyn seems to me to catch precisely both the enormous importance of the classics in the intellectual life of the time and the restricted limits of that importance. "Most conspicuous," says Bailyn, "in the writings of the Revolutionary period was the heritage of classical antiquity. Knowledge of classical authors was universal among colonists with any degree of education, and references to them . . . abound. . . ." He then weighs these references and after some discussion, concludes as follows: "The classics of the ancient world are everywhere in the literature of the Revolution, but . . ." and here is the key phrase, "but they are everywhere illustrative, not determinative, of thought."[5]

To put the role of the classics in eighteenth-century America in perspective it is revealing to look at the major formal educational institutions, colleges, schools, and libraries. They clearly reflect the grip

5. Bernard Bailyn, *The Ideological Origins of the American Revolution* (Cambridge, Mass.: Harvard University Press, 1967), pp. 23–26.

of classical learning. The colonial colleges all made command of the ancient languages *the* requirement for admission. An audience at a women's college in 1978 may or may not be amused at an anecdote that illustrates this fundamental fact. Ezra Stiles, president of Yale in the later eighteenth century, conducted an examination in Greek and Latin of Lucinda Foote, age twelve. He then presented to her a certificate testifying to her being acceptable as a freshman at Yale—if she had been a boy. The grammar schools, that is, high schools or prep schools, were inevitably put under pressure by this universal criterion. Yet they, and the colleges even more so, taught numerous other subjects as well as Greek and Latin. As the eighteenth century progressed, the emphasis upon the sciences becomes conspicuous. In short, the classics are preeminently the foundation. They are one ingredient, albeit an important one, in an education tending toward diversity.[6]

The evidence regarding libraries gives, I think, a valuable insight. Reinhold offers the following notable figures.

Of 417 books given to Yale in 1719 by Elihu Yale, 19 were on classical topics.

When so devoted a classicist as Jefferson recommended titles for the library of Robert Skipwith in 1771, he suggested 140 titles, of which only 16 were on classical subjects.

A 1960 University of Illinois doctoral dissertation analyzing the contents of five college libraries throughout the eighteenth century found the quantitative division by subject to be overall as follows: theological works 50%, history 12–15%, belles lettres 11–15%, science 7–12%, philosophy 3–8%. This breakdown does not, of course, reveal the incidence of ancient materials, but does show something of the emphasis in those libraries. As early as 1700 the stock of the Boston bookseller Richard Perry, who died in that year, was inventoried. Of 6,000 volumes, 300—or 5%—were classical. In the 1750's in Charleston, South Carolina, in a dispute over budget, Christopher Gadsden resigned from the Library Society. His proposal, that 70% of the annual appropriation be expended on Greek and Roman classics, had been rejected when the librarian showed the board that no one had requested the classical works already in the library.[7]

To summarize, the evidence indicates the fundamental place of antiquity in the education and in the reading of eighteenth-century Americans, but it also shows that it was only one among many other areas of knowledge *and not the one most favored*.

6. For the anecdote, see Gummere, *Colonial Mind*, p. 59. For the educational trends, Reinhold, *Classick Pages*, pp. 3–6.

7. The data on libraries are from Reinhold, *Classick Pages*, pp. 6–8, with detailed references.

I should like now to look briefly at the ancient writers who were actually read and cited by the Founding Fathers. It must be admitted that the detailed quantitative study that alone would permit sure generalization has not yet been performed. The assertions I make are therefore impressionistic. I make no pretense to completeness.[8]

For instance, "scientific" writers. Hippocrates, Strabo, Pliny the Elder, Manilius. Except for the legendary Hippocrates, these are not names exactly on the tongue of today's classicists. But the Founding Fathers found them interesting and even, with due caution—for science was well launched on its brilliant modern course—informative. They read and excerpted and cited.

Next, philosophers. The word philosophy, of course, is susceptible of differing usage, and in ordinary discourse, the Founding Fathers, like many of us, found the literature of antiquity *generally* philosophical, that is, instructive, thoughtful. For formal philosophy there appeared to be little taste, unless it was political philosophy. The moral philosophy of later Stoics, like Epictetus and Marcus Aurelius, was much admired, Plato and Aristotle very little. Aristotle held a very high place for his political thought; Plato was held at arm's length. Again and again one cites Jefferson, not necessarily typical but deeply imbued with classical learning, and strongly opinionated. Jefferson's views on Plato are well known, and ferocious: ". . . no writer, ancient or modern," he says, "has bewildered the world with more *ignis fatui* than this renowned philosopher, in ethics, in politics and physics." The contradictory aspects of Socrates Jefferson attributed to "the whimsies of Plato's own foggy brain."[9]

It may be surprising to find Xenophon admired as a philosophic writer. But the philosophical mind that especially appealed to the Founding Fathers was, not surprisingly, that immensely influential writer, the subject of Mr. Stieber's paper, Cicero. Cicero's philosophical writings in essence made the world of Hellenistic Greek philosophy, primarily moral philosophy, accessible to Romans. Since most of the works he explained or paraphrased have not survived, his contribution, while not original, was vast, and was vastly admired by men who found themselves temperamentally in harmony.

Now for the poets. I shall have to content myself with a few remarks, intended to be suggestive. The Founding Fathers evince an acquaintance with the whole range of Greek and Latin poetry, but their favorites are

8. Nor to original research. The factual material that follows, to p. 145, is mainly summarized from Reinhold, *Classick Pages*, pp. 31–151. The opinions are mine.

9. Cited in Louis B. Wright, "Thomas Jefferson and the Classics," *Proceedings of the American Philosophical Society* 87 (1943–1944), p. 229. The judgment is understandably a favorite and is often quoted.

generally Latin, and generally the poets one might call worldly and topical, such as Juvenal and Ovid, and above all Horace. Terence, too, is often cited. Vergil is rated high, Lucretius rarely mentioned.

Writers of fables—Aesop, in particular—were popular. Epistolographers were in far higher repute in that letter-writing era than we telephoners can understand. The two great collections of letters that classical literature provides, those of Cicero—again—and Pliny the Younger, were thoroughly ransacked for sententious thoughts and telling phrases for all occasions.

Next, orators. In a world in which public speaking was frequent and important, the ancient literary art was not merely attended to, it was studied. The famous orators whose works have come down to us served as models. Among the Greeks, Isocrates and Demosthenes were especially admired, among the Romans the inevitable Cicero. Not only orators as such, however, were studied, but also the orations contained in the works of those historians who followed the lead of Thucydides in dramatizing their writings with speeches that might well be fictional but no less excellent for that. Again, almost inevitably, we turn to Jefferson for a pungent opinion on oratory and its ancient practitioners. Although he admired Cicero immensely, it was not for oratory. Perhaps to Jefferson more than to most of his contemporaries, admiration was not idolatry, but highly selective and critical. Here he is on Cicero's oratory: "Speeches measured by the hour die with the hour."[10]

Finally, historians. The giants—or at any rate the writers held in highest regard in *our* time—are read: Herodotus and Thucydides probably exhaust that list. Much more attention, however, was paid to—among the Greeks—Polybius, Diodorus, and Dionysius of Halicarnassus. (Do I hear some classics major say "Dionysius *who*?") It is worth while to consider *why* these writers had so great a success with the Founding Fathers. The reason I think is that they all come late enough to deal with a world in which Romans figure, and Americans found it easier to identify with Romans (rather than with Greeks), and also with the particular vicissitudes of Roman history.

Then there are the Roman historians themselves. Sallust and Livy—all umteen volumes of the latter—were very well known. References to events and persons in their writings could expect to meet with an immediate and quasi-universal recognition. The lesser historians were known too, such writers as Cornelius Nepos. Towering above them all stood Tacitus. Now differences of opinion are always possible, but I do not recall ever to have startled anyone by referring to Tacitus as the best of the Latin historians. He is generally so accepted. That, however, is

10. *Ibid.*, p. 228.

not what Jefferson has to say about him. Brace yourselves for this one. He found Tacitus to be "the first writer in the world without a single exception."[11]

I don't know about you, but *my* students would leave Smith College if asked to read as many pages of Tacitus as they will dutifully, even happily, read in the works of Sophocles or Shakespeare or Homer or Vergil or Dante or even Herodotus and Thucydides. Why was Tacitus so exaggeratedly admired? I believe the answer lies in two facets of Tacitus' work that are very important for our grasp of the Founding Fathers' views. One is that of style. And here it is all-important to read him in the original. Tacitus' is a pungent, epigrammatic style, very brilliant, and notoriously hard to translate without resorting to twice as many words as in the original. As we have already noticed, Jefferson found Cicero too prolix. He particularly admired terse writing, and I think that in that he is typical. The other aspect of Tacitus is political, and it is crucial to our understanding of the thought of the Founding Fathers. Of all the ancient writers who espoused the cause of liberty, of political independence, of republican government, who hated the pretensions and the tyranny of monarchy, Tacitus is the most relentless and singleminded. Those and only those are the themes of his work. And to top it off, he is a moralist. He sees the history of which he writes in the form of the morals and characters of the people who performed it. In this too he strikes a passionate response from the minds of his eighteenth-century American readers. History, for them, was not the systematic search for accurate information for its own sake. It was a great storehouse of moral lessons to be drawn from what men have done in former times. This, as Commager has noted, is what history has been to most people in most ages. Here is how Jefferson goes on, following the accolade to Tacitus noted above: "His book is a compound of history and morality of which we have no other example."[12]

History then tended to be the study of human beings rather than abstract forces, of leaders rather than institutions. The kind of history best suited to this cast of mind is biography and the best kind of biography is that which focusses upon character struggling with circumstance. That is the kind of biography antiquity created, and three of its practitioners whose work was available in substantial amount were especially read, all from the second century A.D., the time of the Roman Empire at its height. One, Diogenes Laërtius, was, in his *Lives of the Philosophers*, limited to intellectuals as his subjects. A second, Suetonius,

11. *Ibid.*

12. Henry Steele Commager, "The American Enlightenment and the Ancient World," *Proceedings Massachusetts Historical Society* 83 (1971), pp. 3–4. Jefferson quoted in Wright, "Thomas Jefferson and the Classics," p. 228.

was, in his *Lives of the Twelve Caesars*, directed toward public figures, but limited to emperors, tyrants, men well worth studying but almost exclusively for their negative traits.

The third was "the incomparable Plutarch," as Reinhold calls him, quoting Cotton Mather. Plutarch's *Parallel Lives of Illustrious Greeks and Romans* provided for the readers of his own time a grand panorama of the famous men who peopled what was already "ancient times." "I am writing," said Plutarch, "not history but lives, . . . using history as a mirror, I try somehow to improve my own life by modelling it upon the virtues of the men I write about." It was a point of view, presented in an amiable and vivid style, that struck a responsive chord for nearly 1800 years, making Plutarch's *Lives* one of the formative books of western civilization. Plutarch was the single most popular classical author in eighteenth-century America, as indeed he had been in the seventeenth century. And his sway was maintained through the nineteenth century, as generations of schoolboys and statesmen saw virtue and vice, success and failure, noble self-sacrifice and craven self-serving, illustrated in the character of public men who were felt to be the heroic forebears of all humanity. As late as 1962, a throwback to that attitude and that morality, the last American President, so far as I can see, who *read* for personal edification and pleasure, Harry Truman, told a reporter that: ". . . I've read Plutarch through many times. . . . I never have figured out how he knew so much. . . . He knew more about politics than all the other writers I've read put together." (Incidentally, the last American President who could actually claim to be a classical scholar was Herbert Hoover.)[13]

The Founding Fathers read more or less avidly in all this ancient literature, but as any student of ancient history can testify, no ancient work nor combination of books will supply a continuous, coherent, understandable presentation of the course of ancient history. For that, modern works, synthesizing the numberless strands into a single narrative account, are necessary. The eighteenth century had its favorites of this kind. With the exception of Gibbon they are no longer read. For those who are interested, I can recommend the samples given by Rein-

13. For the quotations from and about Plutarch, and the continuous high value placed upon his writings, see Reinhold, *Classick Pages*, pp. 39–41 and the notes on pp. 46–47. On President Truman, see Merle Miller, *Plain Speaking: An Oral Biography of Harry S. Truman* (New York: Berkley Publishing Corporation, 1973, 1974), p. 69. Appropriately enough, Miller uses a quotation from Plutarch as a prefatory motto for his book. President Hoover's distinction as a Latinist is attested by his and his wife's translation, with introduction, annotations, and appendices of the Latin work of Georg Agricola, *De re metallica*, first published in 1556. The Hoovers' book was published in 1912, and was reprinted by Dover Publications in 1950.

hold in his *Classick Pages*.[14] They illustrate well enough the bias, the purpose, the value, the tone and content of history as the Founding Fathers read it. In a nutshell, it is Plutarch put in order. The acts of great men, their interaction with the mob, the lessons to be drawn from greed, pride, ambition, patriotism: these are the emphases of the historical writing favored in that time. And although, as I have noted, the Founding Fathers were not lacking in knowledge of and interest in later ages including contemporary affairs, the common coin of educated discourse was antiquity, into which they dipped for slogans, for personalities, for illustrative examples as easily as the children of today cite TV commercials, and with the same expectation of instant and universal comprehension.

I have been trying, in this impressionistic survey, to show some of the particularities of the Founding Fathers' taste. For my major demonstration of the selective use made of the classics I shall present a comparison between the role of the ancient world in the time of the Revolution and its role a decade later in the making of the United States Constitution.[15] In doing so I will be purposing to show the consciously—and unconsciously—selective use to which classical knowledge was put.

In the light of what I have said about the nature of ancient literature, and the attitude of the Founding Fathers toward history, it is not hard to see how appropriate the classical heritage was to the emotional and what we may call propagandistic needs of Revolution. In addition to Latin's being more familiar than Greek to American colonials, the Romans themselves, as I have suggested earlier, seemed closer than Greeks in their attitudes. The Roman experience seemed similar, and the bias of Greece and of Greek literature against one-man rule had become for the Romans an anti-monarchic fanaticism made to order for American sentiments when Independence at last was asserted by the sorely tried subjects of George the Third. The American addiction to Rome, amounting to an identification, to a virtual adoption of the Romans as retroactive ancestors, has been plausibly explained as stemming from the absence of a national history of America's own. True enough, and it is striking to see how references to the heroic past made in, say, the 1820's no longer cite Romans, but our own heroes, Washington, Jefferson, and others. We *had* heroes by *then*. But the peculiar attraction of Rome at the time of the Revolution grew also out of particular circumstances. Roman history was a history of warfare, and although you and I

14. Pp. 155–220.

15. For this material I have drawn heavily on my own unpublished seminar paper, "Classical Influence on the Making of the American Constitution," presented on November 13, 1973, at the Center for the Study of Democratic Institutions, Santa Barbara, California.

may coolly observe that the wars were wars of imperialistic aggression, they are depicted in the ancient historians as the glorious defence of freedom. Similarly the internal chaos of Rome in the last century of the Republic, that is, in the first century B.C., may look to you and me like civil war engendered by greed, class hatred, and military ambition. But some, at least, of the ancient sources depict these scenes as the desperate struggle to maintain liberty in the face of an onrushing tyranny.[16]

It in no way diminishes the genuineness of the Revolutionary Americans' identification of themselves with heroic figures from Roman history to observe that the models were frequently legendary, and those who were historical were heavily idealized. If there is one Roman statesman who stood out as embodying the ideals of loyalty to the Republic, that man is Cato, not the tough old censor who hated Carthage, but his great-grandson, the man who opposed Caesar so strenuously that when finally defeated he killed himself rather than face the humiliation of a pardon from the victorious dictator.[17]

As I indicated earlier, Cicero, with his splendid Republican sentiments, was a favorite writer of the Founding Fathers. Some years before Cato's dramatic end in North Africa in 46 B.C., he had been embroiled in a law court case for which Cicero prepared an oration. The case dealt with scandalous behavior in the family circles of leading Romans, no unusual event. One of Cicero's tasks in his speech was to discredit the hopelessly correct, upright, virtuous Cato, then a young man. Cicero was not averse to slander. But a slander of Cato? Who would believe it? Instead, in his depiction of Cato in the speech *On Behalf of Caelius* Cicero makes mincemeat of him with a fine portrait of a stuffed shirt. The Founding Fathers no doubt knew this malicious piece, but simply chose to ignore it in favor of the Cato found in Plutarch and elsewhere. Plutarch's Cato was entirely ennobling to Republican revolutionaries and one sometimes has the impression he was one of our own. It is that Cato who appears in Joseph Addison's play *Cato*, which was first produced in London in 1713 and enjoyed immense success. Significantly it was George Washington's favorite drama, which he had performed for the entertainment and inspiration of his troops at Valley Forge.[18]

But a decade later, when the task was not righteous war but the making of a constitution, what use Cato now? For the ancient model who was the Revolution's favorite hero there is not the consolation of

16. The adoption of the Romans as ancestors: *inter alios* see Commager, "The American Enlightenment," p. 9. On the citing of native American heroes by the 1820's: Edwin A. Miles, "The Young American Nation and the Classical World," *Journal of the History of Ideas* 35 (1974), 270. The classical source for depiction of Roman civil strife as the struggle for liberty is Cicero, especially in his *Letters*.

17. Bailyn, *The Ideological Origins*, p. 44.

18. Reinhold, *Classick Pages*, pp. 147–151.

even a passing reference in the *Records of the Federal Convention* or the *Federalist Papers*.

Let me look now at the making of the Constitution. Since Gilbert Chinard's article, "Polybius and the American Constitution" in 1940 in the first issue of the *Journal of the History of Ideas*, it has been a truism that the United States Constitution is full of classical influence. Chinard did not claim quite so much. Indeed, his final words claim very little: ". . . the most modern form of government is not unconnected with the political thought and political experience of ancient times."[19] True enough. Also true that the Founding Fathers knew the political writings of Aristotle, Polybius, and Cicero very well, and not merely as filtered through Montesquieu, whom they knew even better. It has been amply shown that the ideas and the categories and the institutions of ancient politics were thoroughly familiar to the Founding Fathers.

But let us see what they actually *did* with these familiar materials. Using the *Records of the Federal Convention of 1787* (the four volumes as edited by Max Farrand)[20] I have done a little counting.

I shall spare you the details, and summarize my findings. There are, absolutely, surprisingly few references to antiquity in the *Records*. Even more surprisingly, relative to references to modern history, those to ancient times are few. A few examples may suffice: there are seventeen references to Rome (any and all aspects), and ten to the Greek Amphictyonic League, the great favorite as a precedent in federal government. These are the largest numbers of ancient institutions referred to. Against them, note eleven references to Switzerland, fifteen to the Holy Roman Empire (Germany), and to Britain fifty-one.

The numbers are suggestive, but let us look at the actual content of the historical references. They turn out, in the majority of instances, to be what *most* people use history for, namely, "Horrible Examples." They are cited precisely as things to avoid. I have been very summary, but I think my point is made: that if the Founding Fathers knew of ancient political experiences and institutions that they admired—and they certainly did—they did not find it relevant to discuss them at the Convention.

If one examines the *Federalist Papers*, the other major source which has been claimed as demonstrating classical influence on the Constitution,[21]

19. P. 58.

20. Max Farrand, ed., *The Records of the Federal Convention of 1787* (rev. ed. in 4 vols.: New Haven and London: Yale University Press, 1966). Vol. IV contains, pp. 127–230, the General Index by David M. Matteson, which, like all such human efforts, is imperfect. I have found a trivial number of references that escaped the index, and no doubt I too have overlooked some.

21. Gummere, *Colonial Mind*, Chap. 10, "The Classical Ancestry of the Constitution";

the situation turns out to be much the same, and not only the situation, but the actual references. This duplication is not surprising in view of the prominence of Hamilton and especially Madison, the chief authors of *The Federalist Papers*, among those who cited ancient material at the Convention.

There are three other major sources that should be examined. One is John Adams' *Defence of the Constitutions of Government of the United States*. I have not done a thorough job on it, but an initial inquiry indicates that as regards classical influence it reveals much the same pattern as that found in the *Records* and *The Federalist*.

The second is the records of the debates in the individual states over the acceptance of the Constitution. No one has done this large task yet.

The third and final source is the Constitution itself. It is often said that embedded in that document is the essence of antiquity's political experience and thought.[22] If so, the essence has been so diluted as to be undetectable at least to my senses. What we are looking for, of course, are institutional terminology, titulature, functional identity.

The attachment of early Americans to the classical world is readily shown in our city-names, our mottoes and our coins, our public buildings, and so on. Howard Mumford Jones in his history of American culture to the 1840's, fills over five pages simply *listing* this sort of material. His paragraph dealing with political and especially with constitutional echoes of antiquity is, however, a disappointment.[23] It could not be otherwise. Very little of explicit ancient reference is to be found. Words like republican, democrat, and Capitol, frequent in our political language, are used in extended or novel meanings, marginal at best to their ancient usage.[24]

In the Constitution itself one might have expected the infatuation of the Founding Fathers with antiquity to have taken the form of a classical nomenclature, with offices and functions echoing the names of ancient offices and titles. Jones gives examples, but they are not to the point, for they illustrate simply the Latin basis of the English language, not the use of ancient political terminology. "Congress" is indeed Latin, but there is

---

Gilbert Chinard, "Polybius and the American Constitution," *Journal of the History of Ideas* 1 (1940), 42, 53–58.

22. See, notably, Chinard, *ibid.*, *passim*, esp. pp. 43, 49, 56; Gummere, *Colonial Mind*, p. 190; Douglass G. Adair, "'Experience Must Be Our Only Guide': History, Democratic Theory, and the United States Constitution," *The Reinterpretation of Early American History*, ed. by R. A. Billington (San Marino: Huntington Library, 1966), p. 130 *et passim*.

23. Howard Mumford Jones, *O Strange New World* (New York: Viking Press, 1964), pp. 228–233. See also Edwin A. Miles, "The Young American Nation," p. 263.

24. These are commonplaces, and the non-classical reader can most readily find the ancient usages by consulting any convenient encyclopedic work such as the *Oxford Classical Dictionary*.

no political body by that name in the Roman Republic nor even in the Empire. The same comment applies to "President." There *are* two ancient Roman political terms in the Constitution, which Jones does well to omit. "Consul" is unblushingly used in its purely modern dress as a commercial representative, a far cry from its familiar ancient meaning, as the highest executive official of the Roman Republic. If you want classical echoes, Napoleon, with his Consulat, did far better than that. The *coup de grâce* is delivered by the word "constitution" itself. Obviously if its ancient meaning, which the Founding Fathers knew well, had mattered to them, they'd have shunned it, for far from meaning the supreme "law" of the people, a "constitutio" in Roman law was a decree issued by the most condemned of all ancient tyrants, the Roman Emperors.[25]

To make a long story short, there is exactly one piece of terminology in the entire Constitution that can be heard as a true echo of its classical ancestry. The "Senate" is the *name* of the most celebrated deliberative body of all antiquity, the Roman Republican institution that a Greek observer referred to in awe as "an assemblage of kings."[26] In the Constitution, however, the Senate appears in name only—not in the method of election, nor qualifications for membership, nor length of service, nor in any of the details that might attest to a real institutional relationship.[27]

Leaving terminology and looking at substance, we shall find the Constitution equally unproductive of ancient references. Look where one will—at powers, duties, eligibility, length of service, election procedure, rotation in office, and so on and on—one will find no ancient institutions embedded therein. Nor is it as if the ancients were lacking in ingenuity or even variety in these matters. The Athenians, for example, had a complex and very clever way of grouping their citizens for election to their Council. The Spartan ephorate was an inventive and unique institution for checking regal power. (It was mentioned, briefly, at the Convention, and summarily rejected.) The Roman assemblies of citizens were organized for voting purposes in three decisively different ways in order to give weight to particular divisions of public opinion. These are but samples.[28]

25. See n. 24.

26. Plutarch, *Lives*: *Pyrrhus* 19.

27. On the Roman Senate A. H. J. Greenidge, *Roman Public Life* (London: Macmillan and Co., 1901), Chap. VI, is still a solid, clear, authoritative, and detailed treatment.

28. There is a substantial literature on each of the ancient political institutions referred to, but a basic description of the Athenian *boule* (council), the Spartan ephorate, and the Roman *comitia* (assemblies) can be found in a work like the *Oxford Classical Dictionary* or, perhaps somewhat less reliably, in any recent textbook of Greek and Roman history. The mention of the ephors was by Gouverneur Morris in the debate of Wednesday, August 15, as reported by Madison.

The Founding Fathers knew these arrangements very well, and could have imitated them had they wished, Why did they not wish?

The answer, I believe, is that they found very little in the classical experience that was relevant to the not theoretical but quite practical matter of making a constitution for Americans in 1787. That might not have been anticipated in 1776, when they were proud to fight their struggle for independence, wrapped, as it were, in a Roman toga.

Even so, *why* was antiquity not relevant? The ancient world had plenty of law-givers, as ancient constitution-makers are called. In the oratory of the Convention and the rhetoric of *The Federalist*, the classical law-givers were passed over almost entirely. In the *Records* only one is referred to, Solon of Athens, one of the Seven Wise Men of Greece, a man so celebrated that even in our own Greekless time his name still survives as a common noun, the headline-writer's short synonym for a legislator. The Solonian constitution in Athens is known (from Plutarch and elsewhere) in substantial detail, and it is a most remarkable piece of ingenious and imaginative compromise with violently opposed views and groups. A constitution-maker might be forgiven for imitating the inspired gimmickry of Solon. In the *Records of the Convention* there are three references to him. Two of them, by different speakers, on different topics, weeks apart, offer the same point, and it has nothing to do with details of his constitution. The gentlemen of the Convention are exhorted to be like Solon, who noted that his government was not the best he could devise, but the best the Athenians would accept. This is Solon the Wise Man, the sage, and the reference to him is noteworthy in being one of the rare approbations of antiquity made at the Convention.[29]

It is the third reference to Solon that is most interesting, and will lead to the answer to my question. Charles Pinckney of South Carolina, in a long speech delivered on June 25 (1787), came to the following point: the people of this country, he said, not only differ from "the inhabitants of any State we are acquainted with in the modern world, but I assert their political situation is distinct from either the people of Greece or Rome or of any state we are acquainted with among the antients." He went on to ask where Solon's "orders" (the four economic classes into which Solon divided the citizen body) are to be found in the United States; "can the military habits and manners of Sparta be assimilated to our habits and manners—are the distinctions of patrician and plebian known among us?"[30] Here is raised explicitly and in concrete form on fundamental matters the question of relevance that lies at the heart of the neglect of antiquity in the framing of the Constitution.

29. Farrand, *The Records of the Federal Convention*, Vol. I, pp. 125, 491.
30. *Ibid.*, Vol. IV, p. 36 (Vol. I, p. 401).

The political ideas of the Revolution, in which the classics were embedded, underwent a remarkable transformation in the decade leading to the Constitution. The classical categories of governmental power and the Polybian statement of the "mixed" constitution,[31] even in their eighteenth-century dress, were at length found to be inadequate for the peculiar, indeed unique, conditions in America. The shortcomings were enormous. I shall note four. One: the absence of monarchy. Two: the absence of an hereditary aristocracy. Three: the fact that all classical political institutions and ideas are posited upon a state which is simply assumed to be all-powerful. The issue of ancient politics is: what group is going to govern? The state, whatever form it then takes, is practically unlimited in the demands it may make upon the citizen. The Founding Fathers were trying to create a state in which the fundamental value would be the liberties of the individual citizens. They wanted a state of very limited power, and one of their major problems was to create a weak state that would nevertheless be strong enough to compete in a world of powerful monarchies and to lead a great people to its already discerned continental destiny.[32]

A fourth and final element may be found to be conclusive in showing the inadequacy of ancient experience: the institution of representation. Those poor experiments of the Greek Leagues with representative government were, charitably viewed, brave efforts. But there is no gainsaying they were simple, indeed primitive, and they were, alas, failures.[33] John Adams, in his *Defence*, written just before the Convention, offers his readers an immense panorama of history, ancient and modern, and explicitly recommends, in an elaborate and quaintly "dated" metaphor, the history of Greece as particularly essential.[34] But his historical survey consists heavily of experiences to be avoided, and his conclusion on the specific point of a federal system, illustrates this clearly:

> The former confederation of the United States was formed upon the model and example of all the Confederacies, ancient and modern, in which the federal council was only a diplomatic body, . . . The magnitude of territory, the population, the wealth and commerce, and especially the rapid growth of the

31. Polybius, *History*, Book VI, 3–18.

32. See, *inter alia*, Henry Nash Smith, *Virgin Land* (Cambridge, Mass., 1950), p. 16.

33. The authoritative works on this subject are J. A. O. Larsen, *Representative Government in Greek and Roman History* (Berkeley and Los Angeles: University of California Press, 1955), and the same author's *Greek Federal States* (Oxford: Clarendon Press, 1968).

34. John Adams, *Defence of the Constitutions of Government of the United States of America* (1787), in Charles Francis Adams, ed., *The Works of John Adams* (10 vols.: Boston: Little and Brown, 1850–1856), Vol. IV, p. 469. *The Defence*, originally published in three volumes, occupies part of Volume IV, all of Volume V, and part of Volume VI in the *Works*, running to a thousand pages altogether.

United States have shown such a government to be inadequate to their wants. . . .

And so, he ends with the call for a "new system."[35]

After the Convention, Madison, himself an assiduous classicizer, in Federalist No. 14, speaks of the new Constitution, the answer to Adams' call, as it were, as a "novelty in the political world"—a "fabric" of government which has "no model on the face of the globe." And James Wilson, a classical scholar who began his career as a Latin instructor, in the ratifying Convention in Pennsylvania asserted an absolute originality for the system on which the Constitution rested, namely "the doctrine of representation altogether unknown to the ancients."[36]

To conclude: the Founding Fathers were steeped in classical antiquity. They loved it. But they were not fools. They knew what was and what was not valuable to them in ancient historical experience.

Let me quote Jefferson one last time. In retrospect, writing to Isaac H. Tiffany on August 26, 1816, here is how it seemed:

So different was the style of society then [in classical antiquity] . . . from what it is now and with us, that I think little edification can be obtained from their writings on the subject of government. They had just ideas on the value of personal liberty, but none at all of the structure of government best calculated to preserve it. . . . The introduction of this new principle of representative democracy has rendered useless almost everything written before on the structure of government; and, in a great measure, relieves our regret, if the political writings of Aristotle . . . have been lost. . . .[37]

There is a persistent tradition dating from antiquity, that persons having the perhaps enviable opportunity to create constitutions always act like graduate students. They run over the world examining the constitutions of other peoples; they study them; and they draw from each its finest elements, creating a marvelous patchwork thereby. The story is told of Solon. It is told of the legendary commission of Romans who wrote the Law of the Twelve Tablets.[38] And it seems to exercise some sway over those who look at the origin of the American Constitution. They have good authority, none other than John Adams, in a grand metaphor that I shall quote: speaking of the constitutional conventions . . .

called without expectation and compelled without previous inclination . . . , suddenly to erect new systems of laws for their future government, they adopted

35. *Ibid.*, Vol. VI, p. 219.

36. The quotation from Federalist 14 is from *The Federalist*, ed., with intro. and notes, by Jacob E. Cooke, Meridian Books edition (Cleveland: World Publishing Co., 1961), pp. 88–89. James Wilson is quoted in Chinard, "Polybius and the American Constitution," p. 52.

37. Quoted in Wright, "Thomas Jefferson and the Classics," p. 230.

38. Livy, *History of Rome*, Book III, 33, 5.

the method of a wise architect in erecting a new palace. . . . They determined to consult . . . all . . . writers of reputation in the art; to examine the most celebrated buildings . . . ; to compare these with the principles of writers; and to inquire how far both the theories and models were founded in nature or created by fancy; and when this was done, so far as their circumstances would allow, to adopt the advantages and reject the inconveniences of all.[39]

In fact, of course, that's not what they did—and the metaphor hides the folly of such an enterprise. In fact, from Solon to Rexford Tugwell, no constitution-maker has *ever* worked that way.[40] The nearest anyone in antiquity ever came, as far as I know, to working up the materials for that kind of approach to the making of a constitution, was Aristotle's famous collection of monographs on the constitutions of 158 separate city-states, one of the lost works of Aristotle that Jefferson wisely refused to mourn. This political theorist's dream collection was lost because no one cared to use it to make the perfect constitution. Even the monograph on Athens did not make it through the Middle Ages, but was found by sheer luck in 1891 on a papyrus from Egypt.[41] Too late for the Founding Fathers, who would have loved it—and left it.

A great modern historian of the American experience, Henry Steele Commager, writing in 1971 about the relation between eighteenth-century Americans and the ancient world, concluded:

So the Americans had it both ways. They drew from the ancient world all the right moral lessons. . . . They drew the names, the mottoes, even the styles. What did they not owe to the ancient world? But at the same time they emancipated themselves from that world, or at least from the limitations which it threatened to impose upon them. They were the creatures of history, but not the prisoners. They were indebted to history, but they triumphed over it.[42]

39. *Defence*, Vol. IV, p. 293.

40. The most extensive source for Solon is Plutarch's *Life*. Rexford G. Tugwell, *The Emerging Constitution* (New York: Harper's Magazine Press, 1974), is an effort, on a heroic scale, to "invent" a new constitution for the United States, one that would be responsive to drastically new circumstances.

41. The original publication of the text: *Aristotle on the Constitution of Athens*, ed. by F. G. Kenyon (London: Trustees of the British Museum, 1891); of a translation: *Aristotle on the Athenian Constitution*, trans., with intro. and notes, by F. G. Kenyon (London: G. Bell and Sons, 1891). The work has since been published many times in new editions and translations.

42. Commager, "The American Enlightenment," p. 15.

HOMER AND THE TWENTIETH CENTURY

Homer and the Twentieth Century

KENNETH CONNELLY

I KNOW OF NO ONE WHO ACCEPTS the doctrine of progress in art today: to most Andy Warhol does not seem a marked improvement over Breughel, nor does Henry Moore seem an evolutionary advance over Michelangelo. All the same, there is something awesome in the widely held opinion that the first poem we possess in the Western literary tradition, Homer's *Iliad*, has never been surpassed as a work of art, that its vision of man and his relationship to his fellows and the universe was the fountainhead of Greek culture, and that our most profound considerations of man and his fate since can be measured against a poem conceived in prehistoric times by a poet about whom we can make a few uneasy suppositions but actually know nothing except that he wrote in Greek, probably in the eighth century before Christ.

The ancient world quite consciously lived in Homer's shadow, or should I say light? His influence on the faith, the ethics, the social life, the entire intellectual and spiritual fabric of the Greeks was immense and pervasive. We need only remember Homer's essential presence behind the Greek tragedians (one recalls that Aeschylus is supposed to have said that he lived off crumbs from the banquet table of Homer) and the poet's necessity to Roman Vergil, whose *Aeneid* cannot be properly read without reference to the *Iliad* and *Odyssey*.

Western Europe, with the ascendency of a pagan-hating church and the loss of Greek, lost direct contact with Homer during the Dark Ages, but with the Renaissance Homer resumed a powerful centrality in Western culture. Let us consider his role in English letters in the most superficial fashion, bypassing his dominance in continental art and thought. The *Iliad* appeared in English translation between 1598 and 1611 in Chapman's "loud and bold" fourteeners which spilled over remarkably into Shakespeare's *Troilus and Cressida*. In 1676 Thomas Hobbes, who might be thought a most unpoetical philosopher, published his version. In the Augustan Age Homer seemed a noble and unavoidable challenge as translations by Denham, Congreve, and Dryden among many others attest. This Augustan dedication reached a climax in one of the major events of English publishing history, Alexander Pope's *Iliad* which appeared between 1715 and 1720. That the Romantics were not untouched by Homer is clear in the untutored Keats's sonnet, *On First Looking into Chapman's Homer*.

> Much have I travell'd in the realms of gold,
> And many goodly states and kingdoms seen;
> Round many western islands have I been
> Which bards in fealty to Apollo hold.
> Oft of one wide expanse had I been told
> That deep-brow'd Homer ruled as his desmesne;
> Yet did I never breathe its pure serene
> Till I heard Chapman speak out loud and bold:
> Then felt I like some watcher of the skies
> When a new planet swims into his ken;
> Or like stout Cortez when with eagle eyes
> He star'd at the Pacific—and all his men
> Look'd at each other with a wild surmise—
> Silent, upon a peak in Darien.

The *Iliad* was translated often in the nineteenth century and Matthew Arnold expresses a prophetic opinion in his Oxford lecture of 1860.

> The study of classical literature is probably on the decline, but whatever may be the fate of this study in general, it is certain that, as instruction spreads and the number of readers increases, attention will be directed more and more to the poetry of Homer, not indeed as a classical course, but as the most important poetical monument existing.

Over a hundred years later Arnold has proved a true prophet. The twentieth century too has had its distinguished translators of Homer—even including Lawrence of Arabia—and the ancient poet is secure at the heart of our literary tradition.

It is false to assume that he survives in his pure and original essence in these countless translations through the ages. Their very abundance is proof that the attempt to recapture that essence is never satisfactory and must be made repeatedly. And, of course, Homer is inevitably transformed to some degree by the temper of his translator and the age in which he lives. The French critic, Paul Mazon, has observed that "each century achieves a solution which conforms to its own conception of art and life with the result that a translator of Homer becomes at the same time a witness to the taste of his epoch." One of the rewards of reading the various translations of Homer through the ages is to see how the gods, the heroic actions, the manners of the Homeric world are transformed to accommodate the convictions of different climates of taste and belief.

With some notable exceptions the tendency throughout the Christian centuries has been to blur the underlying vision of man and his relation to the world which is at the center of the *Iliad*, either by transforming Homeric values as Pope tends to do (Gibbon noted how Pope "improved" the theology of Homer for his audience), or by accepting the unconvincing hypothesis that the pagan vision which sustains the epic can be separated from its art. One read the *Iliad* for its art, not its theology, and admired its ethics at some remove. This sort of Christian reader was the heir of the early Church Fathers who quite properly feared the theological and ethical aspects of Homer. In Milton's *Paradise Regained*, Satan offers Christ on the Mount of Temptation the intellect and beauty of Greece and Our Lord flatly rejects them, and with good reason.

In Thomas De Quincey's autobiography there is an enchanting and telling account of his friendship with an aged Anglican priest. On Sunday evenings under the stained-glass windows of the clergyman's study before a singing of hymns at the pump organ, they would read Homer together. But when the priest saw the imminence of his own death, there was a melancholy last Sunday evening with the sunset faintly lighting the stained glass. A hymn was sung for the last time and the clergyman in tears handed the boy his Homer explaining that it was time to give up worldly things and concentrate upon Christian immortality. Milton and De Quincey's elderly friend were absolutely right in their rejections as Christians who recognized the irreconcilability of the Homeric and Christian views of life.

It is time we looked more closely, if with regrettable brevity, at the *Iliad*, not for its art which has almost always been admired, but for what I might call with some embarrassment and a daring disregard for fashion, its message, the Homeric vision which has been variously assessed through the centuries. It will be my thesis this morning that while the *Iliad* still reigns supreme as art, its vision which tended to be transformed, disregarded, or simply regretted in previous dispensations, now reasserts itself in our century with something more nearly like its original significance and with overwhelming force; the Homeric theology which for so long has been considered evil or irrelevant is now seen by some of our most perceptive thinkers and artists as a touchstone for the modern world. To approach this thesis I would like to contrast what I have called the Homeric vision with that Judaeo-Christian vision which has dominated Western civilization for centuries.

While Homer sang in Greece, the Hebrew shepherd Amos, who may have been his almost exact contemporary, was prophesying to the south in Israel. Amos is the first of the Old Testament prophets whose utterances are preserved. Homer's epics and the book of Amos stand in splendid isolation in the cultural dawn of our world. They were conceived at approximately the same time on the shore of the same sea, but they make clear that in one crucial respect at least, the original genius of the Greek and the Hebrew stood in opposition from the start, for they present two irreconcilable views of the cosmos and man's role within it, initiating a quarrel which has persisted until this day.

In the *Iliad* we are on the fields before Troy where the inescapable essence of life is battle and the role of the warrior is inevitable, where the gods themselves enter on both sides of the fray. How alien to Homer's gods the voice of Amos's Lord seems over the battlefield, damning the battle and threatening to punish the warmaker.

> Thus saith the Lord: For three transgressions of Edom, and for four, I will not turn away the punishment thereof: because he did pursue his brother with the sword, and cast off all pity, and his anger tore perpetually, and he kept his wrath forever. So I will send a fire upon Teman, and it shall devour the strongholds of Bozrah.
>
> Does evil befall a city unless the Lord has done it?

Amos's Lord is the omnipotent, omniscient, one God of the entire cosmos. His supreme claim is righteousness, His Law which will guarantee justice on earth can be known by men, and if it is not obeyed, He will punish the disobedient. All nature is under His rule and every natural calamity and scourge—the plagues and famines, earthquakes and floods—are traceable to the direct exercise of His will, and He uses them to reward the good and punish the evil. Amos therefore lays down implicitly a great philosophy of history which realizes the will of an all-righteous deity. All events and peoples are in God's hand, all political and natural catastrophe must be understood in the light of His justice. And, most importantly, His justice can be readily known and understood by the human mind.

In contrast, the gods of the *Iliad*, Zeus and his squabbling crew, a primitive and discordant household, must seem a sorry divine alternative to Amos's Lord, and there has been no lack of commentators through the ages who have considered the Olympians as crude, insufficient, and discardable deities, perhaps at home in poetic fantasy but no match for the mighty and moral Jehovah.

The God of the Old Testament is a creator, self-mover, and maker of heaven and earth; Zeus creates nothing, is third-generation, and achieves his throne through a particularly nasty form of patricide. Jehovah is omniscient; Zeus is easily duped, by his own wife among others.

Jehovah is omnipotent, His will will be done; Zeus cannot realize some of his deepest wishes and must turn to mysterious golden scales to probe for a truth profounder than he himself knows, and which will never be completely divulged. Above all, Jehovah is the one God, an indivisible unity who guarantees concord and justice on earth if men will obey His command; Zeus is only the greatest of the Olympians who enact a kind of pandemonium as gods who are by their very nature constantly and inevitably at odds with one another. Their existence is predicated upon strife and they have only the most tenuous concern for any human conception of justice which each god sees solely in terms of his and her partial and selfish passions.

Surely no right-thinking human being could fail to see that Jehovah is God as he *ought* to be when contrasted with Zeus and his family. He is justice against caprice, order against chaos, concord against strife, the creator and controller of a universe which makes sense in human terms, where virtue is rewarded, evil punished, and good triumphant. He is ultimately the God we see, however faintly, in Dante's white rose of Paradise. He has, in homelier phrase, the whole world in His hands.

But a cold look at the whole world may give us pause.

Sadly, neither the course of human history since the eighth century B.C. nor the evidence of our own lives affords a convincing proof and demonstration of Amos's exalted vision of divine and human justice. Fifteen hundred years of Christian civilization culminated in Adolf Hitler. The saintly lady at the corner succumbs of intestinal cancer. Strife and injustice, not concord and peace, seem to be central facts of our collective and private lives. The belief in Amos's God demands a tremendous act of faith and a dismissal of the facts of life. The Olympians, on the other hand, stand only too convincingly on twentieth-century soil and could provide the divine machinery, if any were used in our time, for a novelist like Hemingway or Camus or a physicist like Jacques Monod. In sum, we are faced with that crucial distinction between what *ought* to be—and who would deny that Jehovah ought to be God?—and what *is*. Conceivably, these Olympian gods, far from being fanciful creations, are a radiant and cold reflection of the world as we know it.

We may wish for a society in which, in Isaiah's words, "the wolf shall dwell with the lamb," but the consistently predatory beasts of Homer's similes are more believable. The New Testament to many is the culmination of what is implicit in Amos's vision of God, but when we read in Matthew,

> Look at the birds of the air: they neither sow nor reap nor gather into barns, and yet your heavenly Father feeds them,

it may not seem as complete and true a picture as that of Homer's heroes who

> give their bodies to be the delicate feasting
> Of dogs, of birds, and the will of Zeus was accomplished.[1]

The Homeric gods arguably are ways of seeing our world, not as we would have it but as ways of objectifying the dilemma of a tragic universe in which discord is the norm and justice is accidental or only achieved through a remarkable effort of human will quite independent of any divine action. Far from being fanciful inventions, these gods and their attendants can be thought of as a vast and honest mirror reflecting the actual worlds of nature and men. They are all the potentialities of human life—our desire for justice lodged nobly, if tenuously, in the image of Zeus, our visionary aspiration in the beautiful lineaments of Apollo, our resourceful shrewdness in helmeted Athene, our lustful heat in Aphrodite, our chastity in Artemis, our destructiveness in Ares. All the contradictory powers and passions which we possess have taken on anthropomorphic form to act out the patterns of our lives.

As a corollary to this, these gods act within Homer's poems, as some critics have suggested, as psychological metaphors which define and universalize the actions of the characters they visit. These gods do not act against human nature, they do not contradict it. Rather they act through human nature and only visit those mortals in whom in a real sense they exist, characters who are ready for them: Athene spends little time with fools, Aphrodite cannot be excluded from Helen's bedchamber. I am particularly impressed by Athene's visit to Achilles in the first book of the *Iliad* when the hero rashly draws his sword on Agamemnon.

> The goddess standing behind Peleus' son caught him by the fair hair
> appearing to him only, for no man of the others saw her.

This incident stated discursively could be paraphrased, "Achilles used his head," but what is precisely Homeric is that the divine action of Athene catching Achilles's hair reminds one of the instinctive and recognizable physical gesture many of us make when we suddenly think, the hand catching the back of the head.

The fact that these gods contradict each other and stand in inevitable enmity, one to the other as guarantors of strife, tells the truth about our human reality, the conflicts of nations and the conflicts within ourselves with concrete power. To comprehend the Homeric gods it is necessary that we see them outside the framework of good and evil that Hebraic thought erected. In familiar phrase, they are beyond human notions of

1. Quotations from Homer's *Iliad* are from Richmond Lattimore's translation, University of Chicago Press.

good and evil, oblivious to human oughtness and they shine beautifully and terribly and undeniably before us as what is.

In the *Iliad* what we generally separate as good and bad are so inextricably mixed, indeed often so dependent upon one another, that the categories established by Amos seem irrelevant or even destructive when they are forced upon it. Homer falls short of the sort of conviction which allows one to say good Greek, bad Trojan with ease as one might say good Jew, bad Egyptian in the Old Testament. All things are involved in one another and the result is the contradictions which we must accept although they may confound us. Rachel Bespaloff has written penetratingly on this subject.

> Others may blame Zeus and marvel that he permits "the good to be ranked with the bad, those whose souls turn toward justice with those who are given over to violence." With Homer there is no marvelling or blaming, and no answer is expected. Who is good in the *Iliad*? Who is bad? Such distinctions do not exist; there are only men suffering, warriors fighting, some winning, some losing. The passion for justice emerges only in the mourning for justice, in the dumb avowal of silence. To condemn force, or absolve it, would be to condemn, or absolve, life itself.[2]

Homer casts a cold eye on life and finds it inescapably tragic. Goethe understood him when he wrote, "From Homer . . . everyday I learn that in our life here above ground we have, properly speaking, to enact Hell." But it is the Greek poet's glory and triumph that in the face of what should mean despair, he asserts the magnificence and nobility of life, and in one of the most moving scenes in literature—the meeting of Priam and Achilles in Book XXIV of the *Iliad*—dramatizes how a human being may rise above the tragic universe in which he is sentenced to live and die, through the miracle of human love. The *Iliad*, if it confronts us with a universe in many ways negative, finally affirms a very positive life for human beings on earth.

If I have accurately suggested the Homeric vision in these perilously brief and oversimplified remarks, its immediacy and power for the twentieth-century thinker, artist or, indeed, any modern must be obvious. It is a fascinating and endless pursuit to investigate how much of our thought and art is informed, consciously or not, by the Homeric vision. We come nearer to the heart of William Butlet Yeats's imagination which in its complicated and individual way was haunted by Homer from the time of his earliest poems when Oscar Wilde compared Yeats's art to the Greek's. As a young poet he saw Maud Gonne as a reincarnation of Helen of Troy and in his last poems he still can sing,

2. Rachel Bespaloff, *On the Iliad*, translated by Mary McCarthy, Bollingen Series IX, Princeton University Press.

"Homer is my example and his unchristened heart," ultimately reaching his powerful variation of the Homeric vision with his concept of "tragic joy." We read the thinner heroics of Hemingway, whose heroes nobly play a game inevitably lost, in a more meaningful way perhaps if we feel the Homeric resonance behind them.

The affinity of the Homeric vision to that dominant philosophic and literary mode of the twentieth century, existentialism, is striking. The existential premises behind so much modern literature sound like an abstract paraphrase of what Homer has acted out concretely in his epics: that the universe does not make sense from a purely human point of view, that its foundation is obscure (Zeus's scales), that individuals appear face to face with pure contingency which cannot be comprehended within a rational system—these are tenets of existentialism which add up to the desolate doctrine of the absurd which has informed so much of our art. Yet for some existential artists it is possible to make a noble affirmation in the face of this gloomy, pessimistic picture, to assert a real, if limited, magnificence. Some can still believe that man has a choice. The heavens may be cruel and senseless, but he need not be. His intelligence and ability to love, if only momentarily and incompletely, can assert themselves to realize values of human worth. Again and again in contemporary literature we have paler shadows of Priam before Achilles.

The Nobel prize novelist, Albert Camus seems a direct descendant of Homer with his love for Mediterranean clarity, his admiration for the Greek sense of limits, his sense of the absurd universe, and his will that man should rebel against it and struggle for human goodness. In his novel, *The Plague*, the rats which inflict a brutal and senseless epidemic upon the citizens of Oran, the good and bad indiscriminately, are Camus' equivalent of the ultimately senseless warfare of the *Iliad* and in this modern horror, Camus dramatizes men asserting their magnificence. The conventional Judaeo-Christian notions of good and evil held by the character Father Paneloux are confounded, and the scientist Rieux and the quintessential "absurd man," Tarrou, achieve a twentieth-century equivalent of Homer's awareness. Tarrou realizes that all men by their nature and the nature of their world are, however unwillingly and unknowingly, murderers; they are like warriors caught on the unavoidable battleground of the *Iliad*. Tarrou has found murder at the center of his orthodox father's court of law, and the same sort of murder at the heart of a Communist cell he joins in an attempt to escape his father's world. Tarrou's pronouncements are thoroughly Homeric.

As time went on, I merely learned that even those who were better than the rest could not keep themselves nowadays from killing or letting others kill, because such is the logic by which they live; and that we can't stir a finger in this world without bringing death to somebody. . . . I have realized that we all have the plague and I have lost my peace . . . each one of us has the plague within him; and no one, no one on earth is free from it. All I maintain is that on this earth there are pestilences and there are victims, and it's up to us, so far as possible, not to join forces with the pestilences. . . . It comes to this . . . what interests me most is learning to become a saint.[3]

Dr. Rieux reminds Tarrou, "But you don't believe in God." He replies, "Exactly! Can one be a saint without God—that's the problem, in fact the only problem I'm up against today." Almost three thousand years separate Homer and Camus and the Frenchman's thought has been colored by Christianity, but underlying it the Homeric vision is strong and unmistakable.

It would be richly rewarding if we could trace the ubiquitous presence of Homer in modern thought and art, if we could for example, explore a field too vast for this morning's lecture, and follow James Joyce's twentieth-century reincarnation of Ulysses, Leopold Bloom, in "the incertitude of the void." This wonderfully common man affirms human love and the role of compassion in a realistically conceived universe which, despite its seeming distance from the more overtly mythical world of Odysseus, comes to a Homeric understanding. There are innumerable latter-day Homerics but I will finish with the most perceptive and deeply moving of them all, Simone Weil.

What I have called the Homeric vision led Camus to a humanist idealism based upon agnosticism, but another French thinker, Simone Weil, although she accepts Homer as the most accurate depictor of life on earth, uses his terrible mystery as a way toward a mystical affirmation of God. She is a troublesome creature for most of us to ponder, not only because of the tragedy of her end, but because she joined intellectual clarity with an inflexible moral sense, and was at once a philosopher and saint who practiced what she preached with a consistency that shames most of us. Simone was the brilliant, carefully nurtured, indeed pampered, child of a comfortably placed Jewish family in France. Her brother achieved international distinction as a mathematician. She was a brilliant student who among other accomplishments gained a scholarly grasp of Greek literature. Her writings, introduced to most English readers by T. S. Eliot, have earned her an imposing and permanent place in the intellectual and religious history of the twentieth century. With the advent of Hitler, the Weil family necessarily ran for its life. And in this time of terror when she faced the world of the holocaust around her, she turned not to the faith of her fathers but to Homer and wrote her deservedly celebrated essay, *The Iliad or, The Poem of Force*.

3. Albert Camus, *The Plague*, translated by Stuart Gilbert, Modern Library.

The true hero, the true subject, the center of the *Iliad* is force. Force employed by man, force that enslaves man, force before which man's flesh shrinks away. In this work, at all times, the human spirit is shown as modified by its relations with force, as swept away, blinded by the very force it imagined it could handle, as deformed by the weight of the force it submits to. For those dreamers who considered that force, thanks to progress, would some day be a thing of the past, the *Iliad* could appear as an historical document; for others, whose powers of recognition are more acute and perceive force, today as yesterday, at the very center of human history, the *Iliad* is the purest and loveliest of mirrors.

To define force—it is that x which turns anybody who is subjected to it into a *thing*. Exercised to the limit, it turns man into a thing in the most literal sense: it makes a corpse out of him. Somebody was here, and the next minute there is nobody here at all; this is the spectacle that the *Iliad* never wearies of showing us. . . . The bitterness of such a spectacle is offered to us absolutely undiluted. No comforting fiction intervenes; no consoling prospect of immortality; and on the hero's head no washed-out halo of patriotism descends.

Force is as pitiless to the man who possesses it, or thinks he does, as it is to its victims; the second it crushes, the first it intoxicates. The human race is not divided up, in the *Iliad*, into conquered persons, slaves, suppliants, on the one hand, and conquerers and chiefs on the other. In this poem there is not a single man who does not have to bow his neck to force.

Thus violence obliterates anybody who feels its touch. It seems just as external to its employer as to its victim. And from this springs the idea of a destiny before which the executioner and the victim stand equally innocent, before which conquered and conqueror are brothers in the same distress. . . .

A monotonous desolation would result were it not for those few luminous moments, scattered here and there throughout the poem, those brief, celestial moments in which man possesses his soul. The soul that awakes then, to live for an instant only and be lost almost at once in force's vast kingdom, awakes pure and whole; it contains no ambiguities, nothing complicated or turbid; it has no room for anything but courage and love. . . . There is hardly any form of pure love known to humanity of which the *Iliad* does not treat. . . .

But the purest triumph of love, the crowning grace of war, is the friendship that floods the hearts of mortal enemies. Before it a murdered son or a murdered friend no longer cries out for vengeance. Before it—even more miraculous—the distance between benefactor and suppliant, between victor and vanquished, shrinks to nothing.

> But when hunger and thirst had been appeased,
> Then Dardanian Priam fell to admiring Achilles.
> How tall he was, and handsome; he had the face of a god;
> And in his turn Dardanian Priam was admired by Achilles
> Who watched his handsome face and listened to his words.
> And they were satisfied with contemplation of each other. . . .

One is barely aware that the poet is a Greek and not a Trojan. . . . This poem is a miracle. . . .

Only he who had measured the dominion of force, and knows how not to respect it, is capable of love and justice. . . .

Both the Romans and the Hebrews believed themselves to be exempt from the misery which is the common human lot. The Romans saw their country as the nation chosen by destiny to be mistress of the world; with the Hebrews, it was their God who exalted them and they retained their superior position as long as they obeyed him. . . . With the Hebrews, misfortune was a sure indication of sin and hence a legitimate object of contempt; to them, a vanquished enemy was abhorrent to God himself—this is a view which makes cruelty permissible and indeed indispensable. And no text of the Old Testament strikes a note comparable to the note heard in the Greek epic, unless it be certain parts of the book of Job. Throughout twenty centuries of Christianity, the Romans and the Hebrews have been admired, read, imitated, both in deed and word; their masterpieces have yielded an appropriate quotation every time anybody had a crime he wanted to justify. . . .

Nothing the peoples of Europe have produced is worth the first known poem that appeared among them. Perhaps they will yet rediscover the epic genius when they learn that there is no refuge from fate, learn not to admire force, not to hate the enemy, nor to scorn the unfortunate. How soon this will happen is another question.[4]

If it has seemed that the theme of the Alumnae College—the Survival of Antiquity—is finally the concern of academics and aesthetes, let us remember that at the most terrible moment of twentieth-century history, one of its victims turned for meaning to the oldest poem we possess—the *Iliad*.

4. From Simone Weil, *The Iliad or, The Poem of Force*, translated by Mary McCarthy, Pendle Hill.

SMITH COLLEGE STUDIES IN HISTORY

The SMITH COLLEGE STUDIES IN HISTORY, begun in 1915 under the editorship of Sidney B. Fay, has published to date something over sixty books and monographs in various fields of history. The range of subjects has been intentionally wide, including the fields of American and European history, and stretching in time from the Ancient world to the present. The STUDIES has published monographic research as well as critical editions in translation of significant historical documents. Orders for copies or requests for exchange should be addressed to: Order Department, Smith College Library, Northampton, Massachusetts 01063.

VOLUME I: 1915–16

1 Fuller, Grace P. *An Introduction to the History of Connecticut as a Manufacturing State*. (Out of print)
2–3 Webster, Laura J. *The Operation of the Freedmen's Bureau in South Carolina*.(No. 2 out of print, No. 3 in limited supply)
4 Turner, E. R. *Women's Suffrage in New Jersey, 1790–1807*, and Abel, Annie H. *The Cherokee Negotiations of 1822–23*. (Out of print)

VOLUME II: 1916–17

1 Fay, Sidney B. *The Hohenzollern Household and Administration in the Sixteenth Century*. (In limited supply)
2 Bassett, John S., ed. *Correspondence of George Bancroft and Jared Sparks, 1823–1832*.
3 Alexander, Margaret C. *The Development of the Powers of the State Executive in New York*. (In limited supply)
4 Hanna, Mary A. *Trade of the Delaware District Before the Revolution*. (Out of print)

VOLUME III: 1917–18

1 Clune, Mary C. *Joseph Hawley's Criticism of the Constitution of Massachusetts*.
2 Dietz, Frederick C. *Finances of Edward VI and Mary*.
3 Hildt, John C. *The Ministry of Stephen of Perche During the Minority of William II of Sicily*.
4 Lowrey, L. T. *Northern Opinion of Approaching Secession*. (Out of print)
Available: Univ. Microfilms, Inc. O.P. #39708 (In limited supply)

VOLUME IV: 1918–19

1 Laski, Harold J. *The Problem of Administrative Areas.* (Out of print)
2 Fuller, Mary B. *In the Time of Sir John Eliot.*
3 Gray, William D. *A Study of the Life of Hadrian, Prior to his Accession.*
4 Shores, Venila L. *The Hayes-Conkling Controversy, 1877–1879.* (In limited supply)

VOLUME V: 1919–20

1–2 Woodbury, Margaret. *Public Opinion in Philadelphia, 1789–1801.* (Out of print)
3 Fuller, Mary B. *Development of History and Government in Smith College, 1875–1920.* With a List of Publications of the Faculty and Alumnae. (In limited supply)
4 Bailey, Edith A. *Influences Toward Radicalism in Connecticut, 1754–1775.* (Out of print)

VOLUME VI: 1920–21

1–2 Foster, Elizabeth A. *Le Dernier Séjour de J. J. Rousseau à Paris, 1770–1778.* (Out of print)
3 Blanshard, Frances B. *Letters of Ann Gillam Storrow to Jared Sparks.*
4 Bassett, John S., ed. *The Westover Journal of John A. Selden.* (Out of print)

VOLUME VII: 1921–22

1–3 Bassett, John S., ed. *Major Howell Tatum's Journal while Acting Topographical Engineer (1814) to General Jackson.*
4 Miller, Anna E. *Recollections of James Russell Trumbull, Historian of Northampton, Massachusetts.*

VOLUME VIII: 1922–23

1 McKee, Margaret M. *The Ship Subsidy Question in United States Politics.*
2 Dietz, Frederick C. *The Exchequer in Elizabeth's Reign.*
3–4 Bassett, John S., ed. *Letters of Francis Parkman to Pierre Margry.* (Out of print)

VOLUME IX: 1923–24

1–2 Hansen, Marcus L. *German Schemes of Colonization Before 1860.*
3–4 Rippy, J. Fred, and Debo, Angie. *The Historical Background of The American Policy of Isolation.* (Out of print) Available: Univ. Microfilms, Inc. O.P. #39531

VOLUME X: 1924–25

1 Relyea, Pauline S. *Diplomatic Relations Between the United States and Mexico under Porfirio Diaz, 1876–1910.*
2–4 Spahr, Margaret. *The Supreme Court on the Incidence and Effects of Taxation.* (Out of print)

VOLUME XI: 1925–26

1 Knowlton, Daniel C., ed. *The Journal of William H. Crawford.*
2 Stahl, Rose M. *The Ballinger-Pinchot Controversy.*
3 Curti, Merle E. *Austria and the United States, 1848–1852.* (Out of print)
4 Everett, Charles W., ed. *"Anti-Senatica," by Jeremy Bentham.*

VOLUME XII: 1926–27

1–4 Packard, Sidney R. *Miscellaneous Records of the Norman Exchequer, 1199–1204.* (In limited supply)

VOLUME XIII: 1927–28

1–3 Beaglehole, J. C. *Captain Hobson and the New Zealand Company: A Study in Colonial Administration.* (In limited supply)
4 Dietz, Frederick C. *The Receipts and Issues of the Exchequer During the Reigns of James I and Charles I.* (In limited supply)

VOLUME XIV: 1928–29

1–4 Gabel, Leona C. *Benefit of Clergy in England in the Later Middle Ages.* (Out of print) Reprinted in summer 1968 by Octagon Books, Inc. (In limited supply)

VOLUME XV: 1929–30

1–2 Brown, Vera L. *Studies in the History of Spain in the Second Half of the Eighteenth Century.*
3–4 Ramsay, Elizabeth. *The History of Tobacco Production in the Connecticut Valley.* (Out of print)

VOLUME XVI: 1930–31

1–2 Callahan, Ellen E. *Hadley: A Study of the Political Development of a Typical New England Town from the Official Records (1659–1930).* (Out of print)
3–4 Curti, Merle E. *Bryan and World Peace.* (Out of print) Reprinted in summer 1969 by Octagon Books, Inc.

VOLUME XVII: 1931–32

1–4 Schuster, Eunice M. *Native American Anarchism: A Study of Left-Wing American Individualism.* (Out of print) Available: Univ. Microfilms, Inc. O.P. #39625

VOLUME XVIII: 1932–33

1–4 Tolles, Marian D. *A History of French Subsidies to Commercial Aviation.*

VOLUME XIX: 1933–34

1–2 Hunter, Louis C. *Studies in the Economic History of the Ohio Valley.* (Out of print)
3–4 Lumpkin, Katharine D., and Combs, Mabel V. *Plant Abandonment in the Massachusetts Connecticut Valley, 1929–1933. Its Effects on Worker and Community.* (Out of print)

VOLUME XX: 1934–35

1–4 Shlakman, Vera. *Economic History of a Factory Town: A Study of Chicopee, Massachusetts*. (Out of print) Reprinted in fall 1968 by Octagon Books, Inc.

VOLUME XXI: 1935–36

1–4 Hannay, Agnes. *A Chronicle of Industry on the Mill River*. (In limited supply)

VOLUME XXII: 1936–37

1–2 Gragg, Florence A., and Gabel, Leona C. *Commentaries of Pius II*. Bk. I. (In limited supply)

3–4 McColley, Grant. *The Defense of Galileo of Thomas Campanella*. (Out of print)

VOLUME XXIII: 1937–38

1–4 Kistler, Thelma M. *Rise of Railroads in the Connecticut River Valley*. (Out of print)

VOLUME XXIV: 1938–39

1–4 Martin, Margaret E. *Merchants and Trade of the Connecticut River Valley, 1750–1820*. (Out of print)

VOLUME XXV: 1939–40

1–4 Gragg, Florence A., and Gabel, Leona C. *Commentaries of Pius II*. Bks. II and III.

VOLUME XXVI: 1940–41

1–4 Pabst, Margaret Richards. *Agricultural Trends in the Connecticut Valley Region of Massachusetts, 1800–1900*. (In limited supply)

VOLUME XXVII: 1941–42

1–4 Stavrianos, L. S. *Balkan Federation. A History of the Movement Toward Balkan Unity in Modern Times*. (Out of print)

VOLUME XXVIII

Green, Constance McL. *The Role of Women as Production Workers in War Plants in the Connecticut Valley*. 1946.

VOLUME XXIX

Bourland, Caroline B. *The Case of Sancho de Almazan and Juan de la Camara Versus the Crown of Castile and the Town Council of Arenas (1514)*. 1947.

VOLUME XXX

Gragg, Florence A., and Gabel, Leona C. *Commentaries of Pius II*. Bks. IV and V. 1947.

VOLUME XXXI

Chapman, Maybelle Kennedy. *Great Britain and the Bagdad Railway*. 1948. (In limited supply)

VOLUME XXXII

McBee, Alice Eaton, 2nd. *From Utopia to Florence: The Story of a Transcendentalist Community in Northampton, Mass., 1830–1852.* 1947.

VOLUME XXXIII

Deyrup, Felicia J. *Arms Makers of the Connecticut Valley: A Regional Study of the Economic Development of the Small Arms Industry, 1798–1870.* 1948. (Out of print) Available: Univ. Microfilms, Inc. O.P. #25277

VOLUME XXXIV

Bornholdt, Laura. *Baltimore and Early Pan-Americanism.* 1949.

VOLUME XXXV

Gragg, Florence A., and Gabel, Leona C. *The Commentaries of Pius II.* Bks. VI–IX. 1951.

VOLUME XXXVI

Bourland, Caroline B. *The Guild of St. Ambrose or Schoolmasters' Guild of Antwerp 1529–1579.* 1951.

VOLUME XXXVII

Hutner, Frances Cornwall. *The Farr Alpaca Company. A Case Study in Business History.* 1951.

VOLUME XXXVIII

Gordon, Cyrus H. *Smith College Tablets. 110 Cuneiform Texts Selected from the College Collection.* 1952. (Out of print)

VOLUME XXXIX

Geyl, Pieter. *From Ranke to Toynbee.* 1952.

VOLUME XL

Hecht, Jean. *Continental and Colonial Servants in 18th-Century England.* 1954.

VOLUME XLI

Taber, Martha V. H. *A History of the Cutlery Industry in the Connecticut Valley.* 1955.

VOLUME XLII

Cohn-Haft, Louis. *The Public Physicians of Ancient Greece.* 1956. (Out of print)

VOLUME XLIII

Gragg, Florence A., and Gabel, Leona C. *The Commentaries of Pius II.* Bks. X–XIII. 1957.

VOLUME XLIV

Gabel, Leona C., *et al. The Renaissance Reconsidered: A Symposium.* 1964. (In limited supply)

VOLUME XLV

Lehmann, Phyllis W., *et al. A Land Called Crete; A Symposium in Memory of Harriet Boyd Hawes, 1871–1945*. 1967. $5.75.

VOLUME XLVI

Pevsner, Nikolaus. *Robert Willis*. 1970. $2.50. (In limited supply)

VOLUME XLVII

Von Klemperer, Klemens, *et al. Aftermath of Empire; In Honor of Professor Max Salvadori*. 1975. $5.75.

VOLUME XLVIII

Gregory, Justina W., *et al. The Survival of Antiquity*. 1980. $10.00.

PRINTED AT
THE STINEHOUR PRESS
AND THE MERIDEN GRAVURE COMPANY
DESIGNED BY ELLIOT OFFNER